Discover your Ancestors

Regional Research Guidebook

Edited by Andrew Chapman

Discover Your Ancestors Regional Research Guidebook

First published in 2015
Discover Your Ancestors Publishing
www.discoveryourancestors.co.uk

Printed and bound in Great Britain by Acorn Web Offset, Wakefield

ISBN 978-1-911166-01-6

Edited by Andrew Chapman

Writers: Andrew Chapman, Chris Paton, Helen Angove, Susan Ilie
Design: Prepare to Publish Ltd

Sources include:
www.thegenealogist.co.uk
www.visionofbritain.org.uk
www.british-history.ac.uk
www.britishsurnames.co.uk
encyclopedia.jrank.org
en.wikipedia.org

Contents

Introduction

Anyone exploring their family history will probably turn first to the great national collections of data started by the Victorians – the censuses from 1841 onwards, and the civil registration records spanning from 1837 to the present. But it also doesn't take long before various branches of your family history start to become localised – perhaps generations of agricultural labourers in a small rural community, or indeed migrants to one of the big cities or industrial areas looking for work. Family and local history are inextricably intertwined.

Every part of the United Kingdom has its own, distinctive history – not just the major battles and key historical events which may have played out there, but also the smaller details of everyday life which impinged upon the actual lives of our ancestors more directly.

The mineral resources of a county have often dictated its industry, for example, with coal and other mining the obvious examples. Areas with rich, fertile soil have been dominated by crop-growing; others by sheep pasture, often leading to the woollen industry. The latter have often turned out to be some of the wealthier regions, which may have affected your forebears' fortunes. Transport networks are also crucial. These include roads and proximity to big cities, but also having a safe harbour by the sea, or useful navigable waterways inland. And even the climate will have influenced the trades common to an area.

All of these factors narrow down the range of likely trades your ancestors would have plied, and add character to places and local customs, right down to the specifics such as Northampton's famous shoe industry, the paper mills of Hertfordshire and Oxfordshire or the smoked haddock enjoyed by the people of Arbroath.

So you'll soon find yourself turning to region-specific resources. Chief among these may well be the local county record office, where there will be a vast array of archives from the papers of local businesses and landed estates, to studies of local trades and pedigrees compiled by researchers who have preceded you. Don't forget family history societies in the region, too – they typically publish lots of data of local interest, and there will be members who have become experts on sometimes very specific local subjects.

Of course, as your family tree widens back in time, you may find it difficult to visit all the many places you come across in person. Thankfully, modern genealogy benefits enormously from the internet, and armchair travel can still reap great rewards for your research. Data websites such as TheGenealogist.co.uk provide BMDs and Census but also have specific collections of region-focused data which will enable you to trace multiple branches of your tree to one degree or another before you ever need think about jumping in the car. More and more parish records are going online, for example, and you'll find many of these at that site – along with 19th and 20th century trade directories, school registers, poll books, wills and much more – not forgetting those national census and civil registration records we started with. If you're lucky enough to push your family back beyond the 18th and 19th centuries, you'll even find regional collections of medieval visitation reports, registers of freemen and burgesses and chunks of the Domesday Book, for example.

This little book will help you with all of the above. The *Discover Your Ancestors* team has put together a region-by-region guide to the United Kingdom which will give you a flavour of each area's history – some of those 'big picture' events such as the English Civil War or Scottish and Welsh struggles against the English, but also the region-specific events which have helped shape its land and its people. We'll tell you about the common regional occupations your ancestors may have had and developments that may have affected their lives.

Even the question of what is or isn't a county poses problems for research – in this book we've generally used the 'historic counties' of England (see www.county-wise.org.uk for more information on this subject) as those are the names you'll find in parish registers, censuses and so on; but check the contents page as sometimes, for practical reasons, we've used modern terms (such as Cumbria to embrace Westmorland and Cumberland) and modern boundaries (such as the large chunks of Berkshire which are now in Oxfordshire, where you'll find many of their records). For the English county pages, you'll see we've included notes on some of the key changes to the boundaries of the historic counties, including the 1844 reforms which attempted to rationalise the large numbers of historic 'exclaves' (where a chunk of a county was separated from the main part), shared boundaries, and some of the modern administrative reforms. For Scotland and Wales, too, we've listed the different county divisions over time.

We've also put together lists of some of the most common surnames to be found in each area (having removed those which are common everywhere to give more of a sense of those thate are distinctively local). And we've summarised some of the essential tools for your research: these include many of the local-specific resources online mentioned above, as well as places and groups to further both your research and your understanding of the area – local record offices, family history societies and regimental or other military museums, for example.

The British Isles have so much diverse history and character – it's a real pleasure to explore it through your family history, and we hope this book will provide a useful reference tool to keep at hand! ▓

Bedfordshire

Bedfordshire stretches from the chalk ridge of the Chiltern Hills in the south to the broad drainage basin of the River Great Ouse and its tributaries.

In the 9th century it became Danish territory, but it was recovered by King Edward the Elder. The first actual mention of the county came in 1016 when Canute laid waste to the whole shire.

Bedfordshire suffered severely in the civil war of King Stephen's reign and was thrown into the First Barons' War when Bedford Castle was the scene of three sieges before being demolished in 1224. In the English Civil War, the county was one of the foremost in opposing the king.

Owing to its favourable agricultural conditions, up until at least the late 19th century Bedfordshire was predominantly an agricultural rather than a manufacturing county. From the 13th to the 15th century sheep farming flourished, Bedfordshire wool being in demand and plentiful. The chief crop was wheat; near Biggleswade, market gardening supplying London was common. The manufacture of agricultural machinery and implements was a significant source of employment in Bedford and Luton.

Tradition says that the county's renowned straw-plait industry – for making hats – owes its introduction to James I, who transferred, to Luton, a colony of Lorraine plaiters who Mary, Queen of Scots, had settled in Scotland. Even as late as 1911, census data shows straw-plaiting and hat-making among the most common occupations in the county, although it declined due to imports of plaited straw from China and Japan.

Bedfordshire was one of the main centres of the English lace industry from the 16th century to the start of the 20th century, although early records are sparse and claims of the role of Huguenot refugees in the industry are

---

HISTORIC COUNTY BOUNDARIES

1844: Transferred to other counties: part of the hamlet of Tetworth (in the parish of Everton) to Huntingdonshire; part of the parish of Ickleford to Hertfordshire

1844: Transferred from other counties: parts of the parishes of Meppershall and Studham from Hertfordshire; part of the parish of Farndish from Northamptonshire

Parishes across two counties: Beds/Herts - Caddington, Dunstable, Lower Green, Markyate, Pepperstock; Beds/Bucks - Woburn Sands; Beds/Northants - Newton Bromswold

RECORDS

Bedfordshire records available at TheGenealogist.co.uk:

- **Trade directories:** three directories from 1885-1903, plus an 1875 list of **burgesses** in the Borough of Bedford.
- **Parish registers** for three parishes (see www.thegenealogist.co.uk/coverage/parish-records/bedfordshire/).
- **Land owners:** tithe commutation records and maps.
- **Medieval visitations** for 1566, 1582 and 1634.

SURNAMES

Common Bedfordshire names:

1841	1911
COOPER	KING
KING	COOK
COOK	COOPER
ROBINSON	CLARKE
GREEN	ALLEN
ODELL	CLARK
ALLEN	HARRIS
HARRIS	ODELL
COX	CARTER
CARTER	DAY

RESOURCES

- Bedfordshire & Luton Archives and Record Service, www.bedfordshire.gov.uk/archive
- Bedfordshire Family History Society, www.bfhs.org.uk
- Bedfordshire & Hertfordshire Regiment Gallery, www.lutonculture.com/wardown-park-museum/galleries-and-exhibitions/hertfordshire-and-bedfordshire-regiment-gallery/
- Find other resources at www.genuki.org.uk/big/eng/BDF/

unsupported by evidence. In the early 18th century, Daniel Defoe's *A tour thro' the whole island of Great Britain* refers to the extent and quality of Bedfordshire lace manufacture, and the Northampton Militia Lists of 1777 document the number of lacemakers in different parts of the county at that time. As late as the 19th century the lace makers kept 'Cattern's Day' (named after Catherine of Aragon) as the holiday of their craft. In the early years of the 16th century, Catherine had been imprisoned in Ampthill for a short time while divorce proceedings were being taken against her by Henry VIII and another local tradition says that she taught the villagers lacemaking. From the 16th century there are frequent references to the working of 'bone lace' being taught to the children of poor people in workhouses in order that they might earn something towards the cost of their keep.

Sedge mats were made in large quantities along the borders of the Ouse, near Bedford. Local clay has also been used for making Fletton-style bricks in the Marston Vale. In the past gravel was commercially extracted at pits in Newnham, Wyboston and Felmersham.

The principal seats of the nobility and gentry in Bedfordshire include Woburn Abbey, the seat of the Dukes of Bedford, historically the largest landowners in the county; and Luton Hoo, seat of the Marquis of Bute and the birthplace of Anne Boleyn. ✠

Berkshire

At the time of the Norman Conquest, Berkshire formed part of the Earldom of Harold, and supported him staunchly at the Battle of Hastings. This loyalty was punished by very sweeping confiscations, and at the time of the Domesday survey no estates of any importance were left in the hands of Englishmen.

Much of the early history of the county is recorded in the *Chronicles of the Abbey of Abingdon*, which at the time of the survey was second only to the crown in the extent and number of its possessions. The assizes were formerly held at Reading, Abingdon and Newbury.

Owing to its proximity to London, Berkshire has from early times been the scene of frequent military operations. During Alfred the Great's campaign against the Danes, it was the scene of the Battle of Englefield, the Battle of Ashdown and the Battle of Reading. In the Civil War of the 17th century, the royalists had some of their strongest garrisons here, and Reading endured a ten-day siege by the parliamentary forces in 1643. Newbury was the site of two battles, in 1643 and 1644. The Battle of Reading took place in December 1688, the only substantial military action in England during the Glorious Revolution against James II. It ended in a decisive victory for forces loyal to William of Orange and has been celebrated in Reading for hundreds of years afterwards.

The natural advantages of the county have always encouraged agricultural rather than commercial pursuits. The soil is especially adapted for

HISTORIC COUNTY BOUNDARIES

1844: Transferred to other counties: part of the parish of Great Barrington to Gloucestershire; the tithing and chapelry of Little Faringdon (in the parish of Langford), and part of the parish of Shilton to Oxfordshire; the tithing of Oxenwood (in the parish of Shalbourne) to Wiltshire; part of the parish of Inglesham to Wiltshire

1844: Transferred from other counties: part of the parochial chapelry of Hurst (in the parish of Sonning), and parts of the parishes of Shinfield and Wokingham from Wiltshire

1972: The Vale of the White Horse, Abingdon and Didcot became part of Oxfordshire, and Slough joined Berkshire from Buckinghamshire

Parishes across two counties: Berks/Hants - Heath End, Pamber Heath; Berks/Wilts - Shalbourne

RECORDS

Berkshire records at TheGenealogist.co.uk:
- **Trade directories:** nine directories from 1830-1939.
- **Parish registers** for 14 parishes (see www.thegenealogist.co.uk/coverage/parish-records/berkshire/).
- **Land owners:** tithe commutation records and maps.
- **School registers** for Eton, Bradfield College and Wellington College.
- **Medieval visitations** for 1532, 1566, 1623 and 1665-66.
- **Wills and administrations** 1508-1652.

SURNAMES

Common Berkshire names:

1841	1911
GREEN	COX
COX	KING
ALLEN	ALLEN
WHEELER	HARRIS
CARTER	WEBB
WEBB	BUTLER
DAVIS	CARTER
HARRIS	WHEELER
KING	TURNER
FISHER	DAVIS
COOPER	CLARK

RESOURCES

- Berkshire Record Office, Reading, www.berkshirerecordoffice.org.uk
- Berkshire Family History Society, www.berksfhs.org.uk
- The Wardrobe, The Rifles Berkshire and Wiltshire Museum, www.thewardrobe.org.uk
- Find other resources at www.genuki.org.uk/big/eng/BRK/

sheep-farming, and numerous documents testify to the importance and prosperity of the wool trade in the 12th century. At first this trade was confined to the export of the raw material, but the reign of Edward III saw the introduction of the clothing industry, for which the county afterwards became famous. This trade began to decline in the 17th century. The malting industry and the timber trade also flourished in the county until the 19th century. Woollen cloth, sacking, and sail-cloth were formerly made in large quantity, but had already ceased to be of any consequence by the same era.

The only manufacturing centre of significance was Reading, which was principally famous for its biscuit factories (the 1911 census lists around 1400 biscuit factory labourers). Boat-building was also carried on at Reading.

Berkshire has also been known as the Royal County of Berkshire since at least the 19th century because of the presence of Windsor Castle and was recognised as such by the Queen in 1957. In 1974, significant alterations were made to the county's administrative boundaries – the towns of Abingdon, Didcot and Wantage were transferred to Oxfordshire, and Slough was gained from Buckinghamshire – but the traditional boundaries of Berkshire, bordered to the north by the River Thames, were not changed. 🎖

Buckinghamshire

The historic county of Buckinghamshire has been in existence since it was a subdivision of the kingdom of Mercia in the 10th century. It was formed out of about 200 communities that jointly funded a castle in Buckingham, to defend against invading Danes. Aylesbury is known from archaeological digs to date back at least as far as 1500 BC and the Icknield Way, which crosses the county, is pre-Roman in origin. The Roman Watling Street and Akeman Street both cross the county and were important trade routes linking London with other parts of Roman Britain.

The sheer wealth in the county was worthy of note when the Domesday Survey was taken in 1086. Many ancient hunts became the king's property (including Bernwood Forest, Whaddon Chase and Princes Risborough) as did all the wild swans of England – swans were bred for the king in the county.

Henry VIII was also responsible for making Aylesbury the official county town over Buckingham, which he is alleged to have done in order to win favour with Thomas Boleyn so that he could marry his daughter Anne.

In the English Civil War, Buckinghamshire was mostly Parliamentarian, although some pockets of Royalism did exist. The Parliamentarian John Hampden was from Buckinghamshire, known particularly for his significant and successful battle tactics at Aylesbury in 1642.

HISTORIC COUNTY BOUNDARIES

1844: Transferred to other counties: part of the hamlet of Studley (in the parish of Beckley), the parish of Caversfield and part of the chapelry of Stratton Audley (in the parish of Bicester) to Oxfordshire; part of the extra-parochial place of Luffield Abbey to Northamptonshire

1844: Transferred from other counties: the parish of Lillingstone Lovell, the township of Boycott (in the parish of Stowe) and the chapelry of Ackhampstead (in the parish of Lewknor) from Oxfordshire; part of the hamlet of Coleshill (in the parish of Amersham) from Hertfordshire

1972: Slough was transferred administratively to Berkshire

Parishes across two counties: Beds/Bucks – Woburn Sands; Bucks/Herts – Chorleywood; Bucks/Oxon - Ibstone

RECORDS

Bucks records at TheGenealogist.co.uk:
- **Trade directories:** 14 directories from 1830 to 1939.
- **Parish registers** for more than 50 parishes (see www.thegenealogist.co.uk/coverage/parish-records/buckinghamshire/); plus further transcriptions from Chesham, Great Hampden, Walton and Wavenden.
- **Land owners:** tithe commutation records and maps.
- **Medieval visitations** for 1634.

SURNAMES

Common Buckinghamshire names:

1841	1911
KING	KING
STEVENS	HARRIS
GREEN	SAUNDERS
SAUNDERS	STEVENS
COX	CLARKE
TURNER	CLARK
WALKER	COX
HARRIS	PEARCE
ADAMS	CARTER
ADAMS	HILL
COOK	ADAMS

RESOURCES

- Centre for Buckinghamshire Studies, Aylesbury, www.buckscc.gov.uk/leisure-and-culture/centre-for-buckinghamshire-studies/
- Buckinghamshire Family History Society, www.bucksfhs.org.uk
- Buckinghamshire Military Museum, Buckingham, www.bmmt.co.uk
- Find other resources at www.genuki.org.uk/big/eng/BKM/

The Industrial Revolution and the arrival of the railway completely changed the landscape of certain parts of the county. Wolverton in the north (now part of Milton Keynes) became a national centre for railway carriage construction and furniture and paper industries took hold in the south. In the centre of the county, the lace industry was introduced and grew rapidly, giving employment to women and children from poorer families. Furniture is still a significant industry in parts of south Buckinghamshire.

In the early to mid Victorian era a major cholera epidemic and agricultural famine took hold on the farming industry which for centuries had been the stable mainstay for the county. Migration from the county to nearby cities and abroad was at its height at this time, and certain landowners took advantage of the cheaper land on offer that was left behind. One of the county's most influential families, the Rothschilds, arrived in Bucks at this time and they built or renovated a wealth of magnificent houses in the county.

Mass urbanisation of the very north and south of the county took place in the 20th century, which saw the new town of Milton Keynes being formed and Slough becoming heavily urbanised. 🔆

Cambridgeshire

including Huntingdonshire

CAMBS

HUNTS

Modern Cambridgeshire was formed in 1974 from the historic counties of Cambridgeshire, Huntingdonshire, the Isle of Ely and the Soke of Peterborough (the latter was traditionally part of Northamptonshire). It was recorded in the Domesday Book as 'Grantbridgeshire' (after the River Granta).

The Anglo-Saxon Chronicle records the resistance which the shire opposed to the Danish invaders in 1010 when the rest of East Anglia had taken flight.

Until the 19th century the Isle of Ely was an independent 'franchise' in which the bishops exercised separate rule as a 'palatinate', and the Soke of Peterborough had its own, secular jurisdiction. The Isle of Ely was seized by the followers of Simon de Montfort in 1266, but in 1267 was taken by Prince Edward.

Cambridgeshire is historically an agricultural county. The county had a flourishing wool industry in the 14th century, and became noted for its worsted cloths. In the 16th century, barley for malt was grown in large quantities in the south, and the manufacture of willow baskets was carried on in the fen districts. Saffron was extensively cultivated in the 18th century, and paper was manufactured near Sturbridge. Sturbridge fair was at this period reckoned the largest in Europe, the chief articles of merchandise being wool, hops and leather; and the Newmarket races and horse trade were already renowned. Large waste areas were brought

HISTORIC COUNTY BOUNDARIES

1844: Transferred from other counties: part of the hamlet of Tetworth (in the parish of Everton) joined Huntingdonshire from Bedfordshire (part of Tetworth remained an exclave of Huntingdonshire until 1965)

1896: The parish of Swineshead was previously a detached part of Huntingdonshire surrounded by Bedfordshire. It was transferred to Beds in exchange for the parish of Tilbrook

1972: The whole of Huntingdonshire, plus Peterborough (originally in Northamptonshire) and the Isle of Ely joined modern Cambridgeshire

Parishes across two counties: Cambs/Herts - Royston; Cambs/Hunts - Pondersbridge, Papworth St Agnes; Cambs/Lincs - Tydd Gote; Cambs/Norfolk - Emneth, Holly End, Outwell, Upwell, Welney, Wisbech; Cambs/Suffolk - Kennett, Kennett End, Landwade, Newmarket

RECORDS

Cambridgeshire and Huntingdonshire records at TheGenealogist.co.uk:
- **Trade directories:** 6 for Cambs and 2 for Hunts from the mid-19th C to early 20th.
- **Parish registers** for more than 35 Cambs parishes and 4 from Hunts (see www.thegenealogist.co.uk/coverage/parish-records).
- **Land owners:** tithe commutation records and maps for both counties.
- **University registers** for Cambridge.
- **Medieval visitations** for both counties.
- **Wills** for Hunts from 1472-1652.

SURNAMES

Common Cambs and Hunts names:

CAMBS 1841	HUNTS 1841
CHAPMAN	KING
WEBB	ALLEN
GREEN	COX
CARTER	GREEN
KING	HILL
COOPER	RICHARDSON
FULLER	CLARKE
MILLER	WOODS
WARD	JACKSON
DAY	CHAPMAN
WATSON	MASON

RESOURCES

- Cambridgeshire Archives & Local Studies has search rooms in Cambridge (but moving to Ely) and Huntingdon (for Huntingdonshire Archives), www.cambridgeshire.gov.uk/info/20011/archives_archaeology_and_museums/177/archives_and_local_studies/2
- Cambridgeshire Family History Society, www.cfhs.org.uk
- Cambridge University Heraldry & Genealogy Society, www.cam.ac.uk/societies/cuhags
- Fenland Family History Society, www.fenlandfhs.org.uk
- Peterborough & District Family History Society, www.peterborofhs.org.uk
- Huntingdonshire Family History Society, www.huntsfhs.org.uk
- Imperial War Museum Duxford, www.iwm.org.uk/visits/iwm-duxford
- Find other resources at www.genuki.org.uk/big/eng/CAM/ and www.genuki.org.uk/big/eng/HUN/

under cultivation in the 17th century through the drainage of the fen district by Dutchman Cornelius Vermuyden.

The Cambridgeshire Regiment (or Fen Tigers), the county-based army unit, fought in the Boer War and both world wars. Due to the county's flat terrain and proximity to the continent, many airfields were built here for RAF Bomber Command in WW2.

Huntingdonshire was first delimited in Anglo-Saxon times and includes the towns of Huntingdon, St Ives, Godmanchester, St Neots and Ramsey. During the Wars of the Roses Huntingdon was sacked by the Lancastrians. The chief historic family connected with this county were the Cromwells, who held considerable estates in the 16th century. Norman Cross, on the Great North Road, marks the site of the place of confinement of several thousand French soldiers during the Napoleonic wars.

Hunts, too, was predominantly agricultural; the limited extent of manufacture consisted chiefly in brick making, paper making, brewing, malting, tanning, iron founding, lace making and rush work. ⌖

Cheshire

Also known as the County Palatine of Chester, Cheshire was occupied by the Romans for almost 400 years, then formed part of the Anglo-Saxon kingdom of Mercia. Mercian place names can be seen throughout the county often indicated by '-ham', '-burgh' or 'bury'.

The Norman conquest in 1070 saw Cheshire harshly ruled by the occupiers as local people resented the invaders and rebelled. Markets had existed in Chester, Middlewich and Nantwich well before 1066, and subsequently in numerous other towns.

After initial skirmishes in 1642, there was an attempt by Cheshire gentry to keep the county neutral during the civil war. However, Chester was a Royalist stronghold, while the market towns of Stockport, Knutsford, Nantwich, Congleton, Middlewich and Northwich remained in Parliamentarian hands. The strategic position of Cheshire and the port of Chester meant that national commanders could not accept local neutrality and forces ended up clashing in the First Battle of Middlewich in March 1643; there were also sieges at Nantwich and Chester.

At the end of the 18th century, industrialisation of the Lancashire and Manchester mill towns saw Cheshire farms abandoned as workers sought a better living. These lands were absorbed into bigger estates culminating in 98% of Cheshire land belonging to only 26% of the population.

The completion of the Trent and Mersey Canal in 1777 and innovations such as the Anderton Boat Lift allowed Cheshire cheese and salt to become major county exports. Also the silk industry was developing in Macclesfield, triggered by Charles Roe building a watermill in Macclesfield in 1744. The railways came through Cheshire in the 1830s. The Grand Junction Railway was authorised by Parliament in 1833 and designed by George Stephenson and Joseph Locke.

Salt has been long worked in the county; it is obtained from rock salt

HISTORIC COUNTY BOUNDARIES

Parishes across two counties: Cheshire/Flintshire - Threapwood; Cheshire/Lancs - Mossley; Cheshire/Staffs - Balterley Heath, Congleton Edge, Mount Pleasant, Mow Cop

RECORDS

Cheshire records at TheGenealogist.co.uk:
- **Trade directories:** five directories from 1828-1923.
- **Parish registers** for 16 parishes (see www.thegenealogist.co.uk/coverage/parish-records/cheshire/).
- **Land owners:** tithe commutation records, and maps for some parishes.
- Records of **freemen** of Chester, 1392-1805
- **Medieval visitations** from 1580 and 1613.

SURNAMES

Common Cheshire names:

1841	1911
JACKSON	HUGHES
SHAW	JACKSON
BOOTH	CLARKE
WALKER	HARRISON
BURGESS	
COOPER	
HARRISON	

RESOURCES

- Cheshire Archives & Local Studies, Chester, http://archives.cheshire.gov.uk
- Cheshire Family History Society, www.fhsc.org.uk
- North Cheshire Family History Society, www.ncfhs.org.uk
- Cheshire Military Museum, Chester, www.cheshiremilitarymuseum.co.uk
- Find other resources at www.genuki.org.uk/big/eng/CHS/

and saline springs, the principal works being at Nantwich, Northwich, Middlewich and Winsford.

Salt pans and first century brine kilns have all been found around the Roman fort at Northwich. The salt beds beneath Northwich were redis-covered in the 1670 by employees of the local Smith-Barry family, while looking for coal. In the 19th century it became uneconomical to mine salt, so solvent extraction with water was used. Hot water was pumped through the mines that dissolved the salt and the resultant brine was pumped out and the salt extracted – but this process weakened mines and led to land subsidence as mines collapsed.

Salt manufacture has remained one of the principal employers in Middlewich for most of the past 2,000 years, and remains so today. By 1908 there were nine industrial scale salt manufacturers in the town, with a number of open-pan salt works close to the Trent and Mersey Canal. Salt has also been used in the production of Cheshire cheese and in the tanning industry, both industries being consequences of the dairy industry based on the Cheshire Plain around Nantwich.

Coal and ironstone were worked in the districts of Macclesfield and Stockport. There were also manufacturers of cotton, silk and ribbons, carried on chiefly in the eastern towns; and shipbuilding on the Mersey.

Cornwall

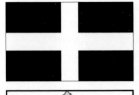

In the early days of its history, Cornwall's geographical position – a peninsula reaching out into the Atlantic Ocean – put it firmly on the ancient maritime trading routes, and it enjoyed a special place in the history of Britain as a centre of trade. The fact that it was surrounded by sea also predestined fishing to become one of the major industries of the region.

In later centuries, however, this topographical quirk became a liability, for a journey from London to Cornwall could take weeks; and despite the mineral richness of the granite batholith on which the county is perched (making its mining industry a matter of national importance) the region lapsed into poverty, isolation and fierce self-sufficiency.

These ironies make Cornwall a fascinating region of study for the family historian. Its importance, combined with its isolation and independence, and its mineral richness combined with its frequent periods of economic depression, created a culture with an unusual degree of depth and integrity, and a remarkably vivid history.

If you have Cornish ancestors, there's a good chance they were miners. The tin industry is perhaps the defining one of Cornwall, but the same geology that produced tin also produced copper, china clay and slate, each of which led to its own industry.

As a result, the Cornish economy was one of the first in the world to industrialise. The Industrial Revolution introduced innovations to mining that brought wealth to Cornwall (for a few) and also brutal poverty. It also, however, brought Methodism, which was embraced by the Cornish and developed with a strong and distinctively egalitarian ethos.

Many people left Cornwall and emigrated to the New World in the wake of the potato famine (less well documented than the famine in

HISTORIC COUNTY BOUNDARIES

1844: Transferred to other counties: part of the parish of Bridgerule to Devon
1844: Transferred from other counties: parts of the parishes of St John, Maker and North Tamerton in Devon

RECORDS

Cornwall records at TheGenealogist.co.uk:

- **Trade directories:** an 1896 guide also covering Devon.
- **Parish registers** for well over 100 parishes (see www.thegenealogist.co.uk/coverage/parish-records/cornwall/).
- **Land owners:** tithe commutation records.
- **Medieval visitations** for 1530, 1573 and 1620.

SURNAMES

Common Cornwall names:

1841	1911
WILLIAMS	WILLIAMS
RICHARDS	RICHARDS
ROWE	ROWE
HARRIS	HARRIS
JAMES	MARTIN
MARTIN	PEARCE
STEPHENS	MITCHELL
PEARCE	STEPHENS
JOHNS	PASCOE
PASCOE	JAMES

RESOURCES

- Cornwall Record Office, Truro and Cornish Studies Library, Redruth, www.cornwall.gov.uk/community-and-living/records-archives-and-cornish-studies
- Cornwall Family History Society, www.cornwallfhs.com
- Cornwall's Regimental Museum, Bodmin, www.cornwalls-regimentalmuseum.org
- Find other resources at www.genuki.org.uk/big/eng/CON/

Ireland, but devastating, nonetheless) and the slumps in the tin industry of the first half of the 19th century. So many miners left Cornwall that it was said "wherever in the world there's a hole in the ground, you will find a Cornishman at the bottom of it".

If not miners, then perhaps your Cornish ancestors were fishermen. The exporting of salted pilchards to the rest of Europe was a staple industry of Cornwall for many years, and is still remembered today in the making of stargazey pie.

The isolation of much of Cornwall's history bred an intense independence. The Cornish often resented the imposition of law and taxes by the far-off English government, but never more so than in the 15th to the 17th centuries, during which time there were several serious Cornish revolts.

Cornish was still spoken natively in parts of the region at least into the 19th century. The disaffection that Cornwall felt with the centralised government of England is probably also responsible for the illegal practices of plundering shipwrecks and smuggling.

By the middle of the 17th century, however, the defeat and loss of life of the previous 200 years of rebellions had taken their toll, and the Cornish no longer tried to defend their identity by force of arms. The unique culture and identity of Cornwall remains strong, however, to this day. ✠

Cumbria
including Cumberland & Westmorland

CUMBRIA

CUMBERLAND

WESTMORLAND

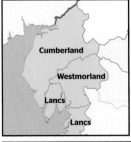

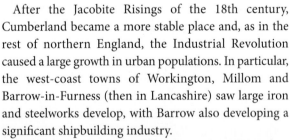

At the end of Roman era in Britain (c410 AD) the inhabitants of this area were native Romano-Britons who spoke Cumbric, related to Old Welsh.

During the Early Middle Ages Cumberland formed the core of the Brythonic kingdom of Rheged. By the end of the 7th century most of Cumberland had been incorporated into the Anglo-Saxon kingdom of Northumbria. Most of modern-day Cumbria was ruled by Scotland at the time of the Norman Conquest of England in 1066 and thus was excluded from the Domesday Book survey of 1086. In 1092 Cumberland was invaded by William II and incorporated into England. The region was dominated by many wars and border skirmishes, and the raids of Border Reivers.

At the time of Domesday Book, parts of Westmorland were considered either to form part of Yorkshire or to be within the separate Kingdom of Strathclyde. The Normans created the baronies of Kendal and Westmorland. Appleby was later the historic county town of Westmorland (Carlisle for Cumberland).

After the Jacobite Risings of the 18th century, Cumberland became a more stable place and, as in the rest of northern England, the Industrial Revolution caused a large growth in urban populations. In particular, the west-coast towns of Workington, Millom and Barrow-in-Furness (then in Lancashire) saw large iron and steelworks develop, with Barrow also developing a significant shipbuilding industry.

Kendal, Keswick and Carlisle all became mill towns, with textiles, pencils and biscuits among the products manufactured in the region.

HISTORIC COUNTY BOUNDARIES

1972: Cumberland, Westmorland and the Furness exclave (North Lonsdale) of Lancashire were fused into the new county of Cumbria

RECORDS

Cumberland and Westmorland records at TheGenealogist.co.uk:

- **Trade directories:** 16 directories from the early 19th to early 20th century.
- **Parish registers** for Moresby, Workington and 5 other parishes in Cumberland, 7 parishes in Westmorland, plus Kirkby in Furness in Lancashire (see www.thegenealogist.co.uk/coverage/parish-records/).
- **Land owners:** tithe commutation records for both counties, and maps for some areas of Westmorland.
- **School registers** for Carlisle Grammar School 1264-1924.

SURNAMES

Common Cumbrian names:

Cumberland 1841	Westmorland 1841
GRAHAM	ATKINSON
BELL	THOMPSON
ARMSTRONG	JACKSON
THOMPSON	RICHARDSON
HODGSON	HARRISON
LITTLE	NICHOLSON
SCOTT	HODGSON
JACKSON	DIXON
DIXON	WILKINSON
NICHOLSON	WALKER
RICHARDSON	SIMPSON
JOHNSTON	AIREY

RESOURCES

- Cumbria Archive Service, with centres in Barrow, Carlisle, Kendal and Whitehaven, www.cumbria.gov.uk/archives
- Cumbria Family History Society, www.cumbriafhs.com
- Furness Family History Society, www.furnessfhs.co.uk
- Cumbria's Museum of Military Life, Carlisle, www.cumbriasmuseumofmilitarylife.org
- Find other resources at www.genuki.org.uk/big/eng/CUL/ and www.genuki.org.uk/big/eng/WES/

Coal and iron were extensively worked in the west of Cumberland, the coalfield stretching from the neighbourhood of Whitehaven to that of Maryport. Plumbago or black lead was obtained in considerable quantities near Keswick. Owing to the general elevation of the land and the moisture of the climate, dairy and sheep farming are more common than arable.

The arable land of Westmorland is mostly confined to the valleys, once known for turnips. Manufacture in Westmorland was confined principally to Kendal (woollens), Milnthorpe and their neighbourhoods.

The early 19th century saw the region gain fame as the Lake Poets and other artists of the romantic movement, such as William Wordsworth and Samuel Taylor Coleridge, were inspired by the Lake District, now the largest National Park in England.

The modern administrative county of Cumbria was created in 1974 from the traditional counties of Cumberland and Westmor(e)land, along with the North Lonsdale or Furness part of Lancashire, sometimes referred to as 'Lancashire North of the Sands' (and, from the West Riding of Yorkshire, the Sedbergh Rural District). ✠

Derbyshire

Derbyshire is punctuated in the north by the Peak District, extending into the Pennines, and by its largest settlement, Derby, in the south. The county also contains the furthest point from the sea in Great Britain.

The Romans were attracted to Derbyshire because of the lead ore in the limestone hills of the area. They settled throughout the county, including near Buxton, famed for its warm springs. Following the Norman conquest, much of the county was subject to the forest laws, protecting game animals and their habitat.

Derbyshire was traditionally divided into six hundreds, Appletree, High Peak, Morleyston and Litchurch, Repton and Gresley, Scarsdale, and Wirksworth. These were based on the seven earlier wapentakes recorded in the Domesday Book, with the merging of Repton and Gresley. Derbyshire came into existence as an administrative division of the Kingdom of Mercia in the mid to late 10th century.

Derbyshire has a mixture of a rural economy in the west, with a former coal-mining economy in the northeast (Bolsover district), the Erewash Valley around Ilkeston and in the south around Swadlincote. The rural landscape varies from arable farmland in the flat lands to the south of Derby, to upland pasture and moorland in the high gritstone uplands of the southern Pennines.

Derbyshire is rich in natural mineral resources such as lead, iron, coal,

HISTORIC COUNTY BOUNDARIES

1844: Transferred to other counties: part of the township of Foston and Scropton (in the parish of Scropton) to Staffordshire

1844: Part of the parish of Glossop on the Cheshire side of the River Etherow was declared to be in Derbyshire – its previous status was uncertain

1884: Three separate detached parts of the parish of Packington, including the chapelry of Snibston, were transferred to Leicestershire

1897: Appleby Magna North, Chilcote, Measham, Oakthorpe and Donisthorpe, Stretton en le Field and Willesley transferred to Leicestershire

1897: The parishes of Netherseal and Overseal were received from Leicestershire

Parishes across two counties: Derbys/Leics – Appleby Magna, Boundary, Donisthorpe, Short Heath, Woodville; Derbys/Notts – Ilkeston, Pleasley Vale; Derbys/Staffs – Edingale

RECORDS

Derbyshire records at TheGenealogist.co.uk:
- **Trade directories:** 11 directories from 1809 to 1941.
- **Parish registers** for more than 70 parishes (see www.thegenealogist.co.uk/coverage/parish-records/derbyshire/).
- **Land owners:** tithe commutation records and maps.
- **School registers** for Repton School (1557-1905) and Derby School (1570-1901), and a 1939 **telephone directory** covering Derby.

SURNAMES

Common Derbyshire names:

1841	1911
WALKER	WALKER
HARRISON	HARRISON
TURNER	TURNER
SHAW	JACKSON
HOLMES	HOLMES
JACKSON	COOPER
COOPER	WARD
FLETCHER	HILL
BENNETT	SHAW
HILL	

RESOURCES

- Derbyshire Record Office, Matlock, www.derbyshire.gov.uk/leisure/record_office/
- Sherwood Foresters/Derbyshire regimental museum, http://www.wfrmuseum.org.uk/derby_collection.htm
- Derbyshire Family History Society, www.dfhs.org.uk
- Chesterfield & District Family History Society, www.cadfhs.org.uk
- Find other Derbyshire resources at www.genuki.org.uk/big/eng/DBY/

and limestone, which have been exploited over a long period – lead, for example, has been mined since Roman times. The limestone outcrops in the central area led to the establishment of large quarries to supply the industries of the surrounding towns with lime for building and steel making and, in the 20th century, cement manufacture. The Industrial Revolution also increased demand for building stone, and from the late 19th century the railways' arrival led to a large number of stone quarries being established. These left their mark on the countryside and quarrying is still a major industry.

Derbyshire's relative remoteness in the late 18th century and an abundance of fast-flowing streams led to a proliferation of the use of water power at the beginning of the Industrial Revolution, following the mills pioneered by Richard Arkwright.

Derbyshire formerly had a detached part in north-western Leicestershire, surrounding Measham and Donisthorpe. This escaped regularisation in 1844, and was incorporated into Leicestershire in 1888. The thin strip of Leicestershire between the exclave and Derbyshire, containing Overseal and Netherseal, is now considered part of Derbyshire. Some parishes in historic Derbyshire, including Dore, Norton and Totley, are now in the City of Sheffield in South Yorkshire. ▒

Devon

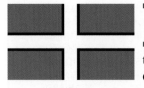

Devon (or Devonshire) was originally the homeland of the Dumnonii Celts and in Anglo-Saxon times was partly assimilated into the Kingdom of Wessex. The western boundary with Cornwall was set at the River Tamar by King Æthelstan in 936 and Devon has been a shire of England since.

Devon has also featured in most of the civil conflicts in England since the Norman conquest, including the Wars of the Roses, Perkin Warbeck's rising in 1497, the Prayer Book Rebellion of 1549, and the English Civil War. The arrival of William of Orange to launch the Glorious Revolution of 1688 took place at Brixham.

Devon has produced tin, copper and other metals from ancient times. Devon's tin miners enjoyed a substantial degree of independence through its Stannary Parliament, which met on Dartmoor and dates back to the 12th century. The parliament maintained its own gaol at Lydford and had a brutal reputation. The last recorded sitting was in 1748.

Cold winters were a feature of the 17th century, that of 1676 being particularly hard. Smallpox epidemics occurred in the 1640s, 1710s and 1760s, resulting in many deaths.

Until about 1300 Devon produced more tin than Cornwall but production declined with the opening of the deep Cornish mines. Tin was found largely on Dartmoor's granite heights, and copper in the areas around it. The Dartmoor tin-mining industry thrived right through to the first half of the 20th century. In the 18th century, Devon Great Consols mine (near Tavistock) was believed to be the largest copper mine in the world.

Agriculture has been an important industry in Devon since the 19th

BOUNDARY CHANGES

1844: Transferred to other counties: parts of the parishes of Make, St John and North Tamerton to Cornwall; the parish of Thorncombe to Dorset

1844: Transferred from other counties: part of the parish of Axminster, and the parish of Stockland (including the hamlet of Dalwood) from Dorset; part of the parish of Bridgerule from Cornwall

Parishes across two counties: Devon/Dorset – Churchill, Smallridge; Devon/Somerset – Bishopswood, Malmsmead, Oldways End

RECORDS

Devon records at TheGenealogist.co.uk:
- **Trade directories:** four directories from 1765 to 1937.
- **Parish registers** for more than 25 parishes (see www.thegenealogist.co.uk/coverage/parish-records/devon/); transcriptions from Parkham and Hemyock.
- **Land owners:** tithe commutation records.
- **Wills:** a collection of transcribed wills from 1559 to 1799.
- **School registers** for Blundell's School in Tiverton, and medieval **visitations** of the county from 1531, 1564 and 1620.

SURNAMES

Common Devon names:

1841	1911
HARRIS	HARRIS
HILL	TUCKER
TUCKER	HILL
BAKER	MARTIN
WEBBER	BAKER
MARTIN	WEBBER
RICHARDS	RICHARDS
COLE	ROWE
HOOPER	DAVEY
LEE	COLE
DAVEY	PHILLIPS
SANDERS	TURNER
BOWDEN	BOWDEN

RESOURCES

- Devon Record Office, Exeter (plus a branch in Barnstaple), www.devon.gov.uk/record_office
- Plymouth & West Devon Record Office, www.plymouth.gov.uk/archives
- Devon Family History Society, www.devonfhs.org.uk
- Devonshire & Dorset Regiment at The Keep Military Museum, Dorchester, Dorset, www.keepmilitarymuseum.org/history/1958-2007/devonshire+and+dorset+regiment
- Find other Devon resources at http://genuki.cs.ncl.ac.uk/DEV/

century. Since the rise of seaside resorts with the arrival of the railways in the 19th century, Devon's economy has been heavily reliant on tourism.

In the later 19th and early 20th centuries there were a number of potteries in the county, mainly based around Torquay in the south (for instance Aller Vale Pottery), and Barnstaple in the north. At first these made high-quality art pottery, but later declined to the manufacture of mass-produced items for the tourist industry.

Census data shows the dominance of agriculture in the 19th century. In 1841, other common trades included fishing and lace making; by 1911, domestic service had become more common. The population between these years only rose from 533,000 to 707,000.

In the modern period, after 1650, the City of Plymouth has had a large growth becoming the largest city in Devon, mainly due to the naval base at Devonport on its west. Plymouth played an important role as a naval port in both world wars. South Devon was a training and assembly area during WW2 for the D-Day landings. Both Plymouth and Exeter suffered badly from bombing during the war. ✠

Dorset

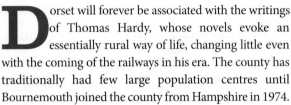

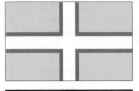

Dorset will forever be associated with the writings of Thomas Hardy, whose novels evoke an essentially rural way of life, changing little even with the coming of the railways in his era. The county has traditionally had few large population centres until Bournemouth joined the county from Hampshire in 1974.

The Vikings raided in the 8th century. After the Norman conquest in 1066, feudal rule was established in Dorset and the bulk of the land was divided between the Crown and ecclesiastical institutions. Over the next 200 years Dorset's population grew substantially and additional land was enclosed for farming to provide the extra food required. The devastating Black Death arrived in England here, at Melcombe Regis in 1348.

Although a quiet, rural area, Dorset has seen much civil unrest: during the English Civil War an uprising of vigilantes was crushed by Cromwell's forces in a pitched battle near Shaftesbury; the Duke of Monmouth's doomed rebellion began at Lyme Regis (followed by Judge Jeffreys' famous Bloody Assizes in Dorchester to punish the rebels); and a group of farm labourers (the Tolpuddle Martyrs) was instrumental in the formation of the trade union movement.

The Dorsetshire Regiment was the first British unit to face a gas attack during World War One and they sustained particularly heavy losses at the Battle of the Somme.

During World War Two, Dorset was heavily involved in the preparations for the invasion of Normandy and the large harbours of Portland and Poole were two of the main embarkation points on D-Day.

HISTORIC COUNTY BOUNDARIES

1844: Transferred to other counties: part of the parish of Axminster, and the parish of Stockland (including the hamlet of Dalwood), to Devon

1844: Transferred from other counties: the parish of Holwell from Somerset; the parish of Thorncombe from Devon

1972: Bournemouth and Christchurch joined Dorset from Hampshire

Parishes across two counties: Devon/Dorset – Churchill, Smallridge; Dorset/Hants – Lower Daggons, Northbourne, Trickett's Cross, Woolsbridge; Dorset/Somerset – Chard Junction; Dorset/Wilts – Queen Oak

RECORDS

Dorset records at TheGenealogist.co.uk:

- **Trade directories:** seven trade directories for the county, spanning 1865 to 1935
- **Parish registers** for more than 60 parishes (see www.thegenealogist.co.uk/coverage/parish-records/dorset/).
- **Land owners:** tithe commutation records.
- An index of Dorset **wills** from 1500-1799.
- **School registers** for Weymouth College from 1863 to 1923.

SURNAMES

Common Dorset names:

1841	1911
BARTLETT	LEGG
COX	BARTLETT
STONE	STONE
DAVIS	COX
LEGG	HUNT
READ	KING
BAKER	DAVIS
HUNT	MILLER
GREEN	HARRIS
BISHOP	BAKER

RESOURCES

- Dorset History Centre, www.dorsetforyou.com/dorsethistorycentre
- Dorset Family History Society, www.dorsetfhs.org.uk
- Devonshire & Dorset Regiment at The Keep Military Museum, Dorchester, Dorset, www.keepmilitarymuseum.org/history/1958-2007/devonshire+and+dorset+regiment
- Find other Dorset resources at www.genuki.org.uk/big/eng/DOR/

The wool trade, the quarrying of Purbeck Marble and the busy ports of Weymouth, Melcombe Regis, Lyme Regis and Bridport brought prosperity to the county. During the 18th century, much smuggling took place along the Dorset coast; its coves, caves and sandy beaches provided opportunities for gangs such as the Hawkhursts to stealthily bring smuggled goods ashore. Poole became Dorset's busiest port and established prosperous trade links with the fisheries of Newfoundland which supported cloth, rope and net manufacturing industries in the surrounding towns and villages. However, the Industrial Revolution largely bypassed Dorset which lacked coal resources and as a consequence the county remained predominantly agricultural.

The county now relies heavily on tourism for its local economy, although even this has a heritage in the county: George III paid frequent visits to Weymouth and popularised the area as a tourist destination.

Census data reflects the county's agricultural history. In 1841, around 15,000 people were listed as 'agricultural labourer' in the census, and most other trades in the top 20 reflect this economy: farmer, carpenter, blacksmith, yeoman, baker, butcher. Mason also appears – the original trade of Thomas Hardy, of course – along with mariner, reflecting the importance of fishing to a coastal county. ✠

Durham, County

County Durham has a mixture of mining and farming heritage, as well as a strong railway industry, particularly in the southeast of the county in Darlington, Shildon and Stockton. Its economy was historically based on coal and iron mining.

The 'County Palatine of Durham' was originally a 'liberty' – in which rights normally reserved to the king had been devolved into private hands – under the control of the Bishops of Durham. The crown regarded Durham as falling within Northumberland until the late 13th century but by the 14th century it was effectively a private shire, with the bishop appointing his own sheriff.

During the Wars of the Roses, Henry VI passed through Durham. On the outbreak of the Civil War, Durham inclined to support the cause of Parliament, and in 1640 the high sheriff of the palatinate guaranteed to supply the Scottish army with provisions during their stay in the county. In 1642 the Earl of Newcastle formed the western counties into an association for the King's service, but in 1644 the palatinate was again overrun by the Scottish army, and after the Battle of Marston Moor fell entirely into the hands of Parliament. In 1646 the palatinate was formally abolished. It was revived, however, after the Restoration, and continued with much the same power until 1836.

At its height, the mining industry – which began in medieval times – employed almost the whole of the non-agricultural population, with large numbers of pit villages being founded throughout the county. The North East Mining Archive can be found at the University of Sunderland and has resources for family historians – see http://bit.ly/1hTtw6i, and Durham Mining Museum at www.dmm.org.uk. Richard II had granted to the inhabitants of Durham licence to export the produce of the mines, the

---

HISTORIC COUNTY BOUNDARIES

1844: Transferred to other counties: Islandshire (consisting of the chapelry of Ancroft, part of the parish of Belford, the township of Holy Island, the chapelry of Kyloe, the extra-parochial place of Monks House and the chapelry of Tweedmouth), Bedling-tonshire (the parish of Bedlington), Norhamshire (the parish of Norham) and the extra parochial Farne Islands all transferred to Northumberland; Craikshire (the parish of Crayke) to the North Riding of Yorkshire

RECORDS

Durham records at TheGenealogist.co.uk:
- **Trade directories:** three directories from 1827, 1834 and 1894.
- **Parish registers** for nearly 20 parishes (see www.thegenealogist.co.uk/ coverage/parish-records/durham/); transcriptions spanning the 16th to 19th centuries from several printed books, including Durham cathedral registers.
- **Land owners:** tithe commutation records and maps.
- **School registers** for Durham School covering 1840-1912

SURNAMES

Common Durham names:

1841	1911
THOMPSON	THOMPSON
ROBSON	BELL
WATSON	ROBSON
BELL	WATSON
RICHARDSON	RICHARDSON
SCOTT	SCOTT
YOUNG	WALKER
DIXON	ARMSTRONG
ATKINSON	DIXON
HARRISON	WILKINSON

RESOURCES

- Durham County Record Office, Durham, www.durhamrecordoffice.org.uk
- Northumberland & Durham Family History Society, www.ndfhs.org.uk
- Cleveland, North Yorkshire & South Durham Family History Society, www.clevelandfhs.org.uk
- Durham Light Infantry Museum, Durham, www.dlidurham.org.uk
- Find other Durham resources at www.genuki.org.uk/big/eng/DUR/

majority being transported from the Port of Sunderland complex which was constructed in the 1850s. The culture of coal mining found expression in the Durham Miners' Gala, which was first held in 1871.

Census data reveals that in 1841, when the total population was just 322,000, agricultural labourer was the most common occupation, and farmer not far behind, but coal and lead miners also featured prominently in the top 20. The proportion of the population working in agriculture fell from around 6% in 1851 to 1% in 1951. There were 15,202 people employed in coal mining in 1841, rising to a peak of 157,837 in 1921.

By 1911, when the population had shot up to 1.4 million (large towns such as Gateshead and Sunderland were once in the county), agriculture has fallen notably down the list. In contrast, the number of people in mining-related trades in the top 20 occupations has increased almost tenfold.

Among other early industries lead mining was carried on in the western part of the county, and mustard was extensively cultivated. Gateshead had a considerable tanning trade and shipbuilding was undertaken at Sunderland, claimed to be the largest shipbuilding town in the world in the 19th and early 20th centuries. ✠

Essex

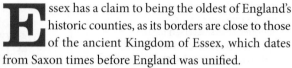

Essex has a claim to being the oldest of England's historic counties, as its borders are close to those of the ancient Kingdom of Essex, which dates from Saxon times before England was unified.

It also claims to have the oldest recorded town in the country: Colchester, which pre-dates Roman times and even once had its own mint.

In AD 825 it became part of the Kingdom of Wessex and was later ceded under the Treaty of Wedmore to the Danelaw under the Kingdom of East Anglia. In AD 991 the Battle of Maldon resulted in complete defeat of the Anglo-Saxons by the Vikings, and is commemorated in the early poem 'The Battle of Maldon'.

Being a relatively stone-less county, it is unsurprising that some of the earliest examples of the mediaeval revival of brick-making can be found in Essex; Layer Marney Tower, Ingatestone Hall, and numerous parish churches exhibit the brickmakers' and bricklayers' skills.

Mediaeval gothic architecture in timber, brick, rubble, and stone is to be found all over Essex, including the large churches at Chelmsford, Saffron Walden and Thaxted.

While the shortened remnant of Waltham Abbey was considered as a potential cathedral, elevation of the large parish church at Chelmsford was eventually preferred because of its location at the centre of the new diocese of Essex c1908. Waltham Abbey remains the county's most impressive piece of mediaeval architecture.

Traditionally the county has been dominated by agriculture, both arable and sheep farming, with the wool trade making the area between

HISTORIC COUNTY BOUNDARIES

1889: Small areas were moved to Hertfordshire, Cambridgeshire and Suffolk.
1965: Various parts of the county also became part of Greater London in 1965, in the present boroughs of Barking, Havering, Newham, Redbridge and Waltham Forest.
Parishes across two counties: Essex/Suffolk - Haverhill

RECORDS

Essex records at TheGenealogist.co.uk:

- **Trade directories:** two Post Office directories, from 1862 and 1878, and Kelly's Directory for the county for five different years between 1886 and 1929.
- **Parish registers** for nearly 70 parishes (see www.thegenealogist.co.uk/coverage/parish-records/essex/); plus transcriptions from Lambourne.
- **Land owners:** tithe commutation records and some tithe maps.
- Colchester **school registers** 1637-1740
- **regimental records** of the 1st Battalion of the Essex Regiment from 1740 to 1919.

SURNAMES

Common Essex names:

1841	1881
TURNER	GREEN
GREEN	TURNER
KING	KING
COOK	COOK
CARTER	BAKER
BARKER	CARTER
BAKER	MARTIN
PERRY	HARVEY
CHAPMAN	CHAPMAN
HARVEY	HARRIS
WEBB	CLARKE
NEWMAN	PERRY

RESOURCES

- Essex Record Office, Chelmsford, seax.essexcc.gov.uk
- Essex Society for Family History, www.esfh.org.uk
- Essex Regiment Museum, Chelmsford, www.chelmsford.gov.uk/essexregimentmuseum
- www.historyhouse. co.uk offers a wide variety of historical information about Essex
- Find other resources at www.genuki.org.uk/big/eng/ESS/

Braintree and Colchester particularly prosperous – many of painter John Constable's most famous scenes come from this area.

Census analysis reveals that in 1841 14% of people in the county were agricultural labourers. Traditional rural trades such as farmer, blacksmith and miller were also common – as were bricklayers, reflecting the importance of the brickmaking industry in the area.

The coast was important, too: Tilbury was a major port for London, Barking once had the world's largest fishing fleet, and of course places such as Southend, Frinton and Clacton became popular resorts. The 1841 census lists more than 1000 mariners in the county.

Much of the development of the county was caused by the railway. By 1843 the Eastern Counties Railway had connected Bishopsgate station in London with Brentwood and Colchester. By 1884 the London, Tilbury and Southend Railway had connected Fenchurch Street railway station in the City of London to Grays, Tilbury, Southend-on-Sea and Shoebury-ness. Some of the railways were built primarily to transport goods but some were to cater for commuter traffic; they unintentially created the holiday resorts mentioned above. ⚔

Gloucestershire

The region now known as Gloucestershire was originally inhabited by Brythonic peoples (ancestors of the Welsh and other British Celtic peoples) in the Iron Age and Roman periods. In the final quarter of the 6th century, the Saxons of Wessex began to establish control over the area. Gloucestershire probably originated as a shire in the 10th century; towards the close of the 11th century, the boundaries were readjusted to include Winchcombeshire, previously a county by itself, and at the same time the forest district between the Wye and the Severn was added to Gloucestershire.

In the barons' war of the reign of Henry III, Gloucester was garrisoned for Simon de Montfort, but was captured by Prince Edward in 1265; in the same year de Montfort was killed at Evesham. Bristol – formerly in this county – and Gloucester actively supported the Yorkist cause during the Wars of the Roses. In the religious struggles of the 16th century Gloucester showed strong Protestant sympathy, and in the reign of Mary, Bishop Hooper was sent to Gloucester to be burnt as a warning to the county. The same Puritan leanings induced the county to support the Parliamentary cause in the civil war of the 17th century. In 1643 Bristol and Cirencester were captured by the Royalists, but the latter was recovered in the same year and Bristol in 1645.

HISTORIC COUNTY BOUNDARIES

1844: Transferred to other counties: the parishes of Little Compton and Sutton-under-Brailes to Warwickshire; the township of Lea Lower (in the parish of Lea) to Herefordshire; the parish of Minety to Wiltshire; the parishes of Shenington and Widford to Oxfordshire

1844: Transferred from other counties: the hamlets of Alstone and Little Washbourne (both in the parish of Overbury) and the parish of Icomb (including the hamlet of Church Icomb) from Worcestershire; part of the parish of Great Barrington from Berkshire; part of the parish of Broughton Poggs in Oxfordshire; the parishes of Kingswood and Poulton from Wiltshire

1931: The county's boundaries with Warwickshire and Worcestershire were realigned, removing the narrow salients from Gloucestershire; in compensation, Gloucestershire gained a number of detached Worcestershire parishes.

Parishes across two counties: Gloucs/Herefords – Clifford's Mesne, Dancing Green, Lea Line; Gloucs/Worcs – Honeybourne

RECORDS

Gloucs records at TheGenealogist.co.uk:
- **Trade directories:** 12 directories from 1793 to 1933.
- **Parish registers** for more than 350 parishes (see www.thegenealogist.co.uk/coverage/parish-records/gloucestershire/); plus some Catholic and Huguenot records.
- **Land owners:** tithe commutation records.
- **School registers** for Cheltenham College and Wycliffe in Stonehouse.
- **Medieval visitations** from 1682 and 1683.
- Bristol **wills** 1572-1792 and Gloucestershire wills 1660-1800.

SURNAMES

Common Gloucestershire names:

1841	1911
DAVIS	DAVIS
HARRIS	HARRIS
JAMES	LEWIS
MORGAN	HILL
WEBB	JAMES
COOK	COOK
HILL	WEBB
COX	BENNETT
PRICE	BAKER

RESOURCES

- Gloucestershire Archives, Gloucester, www.gloucestershire.gov.uk/archives/
- Bristol Record Office, www.bristolmuseums.org.uk/bristol-record-office
- Gloucestershire Family History Society, www.gfhs.org.uk
- Bristol & Avon Family History Society, www.bafhs.org.uk
- Soldiers of Gloucestershire Museum, Gloucester, soldiersofglos.com
- Find other resources at www.genuki.org.uk/big/eng/GLS/

Bristol was made a county in 1425, and in 1483 Richard III made Gloucester an independent county, adding to it the hundreds of Dudston and Kings Barton. The latter were reunited to Gloucestershire in 1673, but the cities of Bristol and Gloucester continued to rank as independent counties, with separate jurisdiction, county rate and assizes.

The physical characteristics of the three natural divisions of Gloucestershire have given rise in each to a particular industry. The forest district, until the development of the Sussex mines in the 16th century, was the chief iron producing area of the kingdom, the mines having been worked in Roman times, while the abundance of timber gave rise to numerous tanneries and to an important shipbuilding trade.

The agricultural hill district gradually absorbed the woollen trade from the big towns, which now devoted themselves almost entirely to foreign commerce. Silkweaving was introduced in the 17th century, and was especially prosperous in the Stroud valley. The abundance of clay and building-stone in the county gave rise to considerable manufactures of brick, tiles and pottery. Numerous minor industries sprang up in the 17th and 18th centuries, such as flax-growing and the manufacture of pins, buttons, lace, stockings, rope and sailcloth. ✠

Hampshire

including Isle of Wight

For several centuries Hampshire's county town of Winchester was a more important settlement than London. In Roman times, as Venta, it became the capital of the Belgae in Britain. After the Romans, Hampshire emerged as the centre of what was to become the most powerful kingdom in Britain, the Kingdom of Wessex.

By the Norman conquest, London had finally overtaken Winchester as the largest city in England, but it remained a city of importance. From the 12th century the county's ports grew in importance, fuelled by trade with the continent, wool and cloth manufacture in the county, and the fishing industry, and a shipbuilding industry was established. By 1523 at the latest, the population of Southampton had outstripped that of Winchester.

Over several centuries a series of castles and forts was constructed along the coast of the Solent to defend the harbours at Southampton and Portsmouth. These include the Roman Portchester Castle which overlooks Portsmouth Harbour, and a series of forts built by Henry VIII. Southampton and Portsmouth remained important harbours when rivals such as Poole and Bristol declined, as they are among the few locations that combine shelter with deep water. Southampton has been host to many famous ships, including the Mayflower and the Titanic, the latter being staffed largely by natives of Southampton.

Hampshire played a crucial role in World War Two due to the large Royal Navy naval base at Portsmouth and the army camp at Aldershot.

HISTORIC COUNTY BOUNDARIES

1844: The tithings of North Ambersham and South Ambersham (both in the parish of Steep) and part of the parish of Rogate transferred to Sussex

1890: The Isle of Wight was separated from the historic county of Hampshire to form an administrative county

1972: Bournemouth and Christchurch joined Dorset from Hampshire

Parishes across two counties: Berks/Hants - Heath End, Pamber Heath; Dorset/Hants - Lower Daggons, Northbourne, Trickett's Cross, Woolsbridge; Hants/Sussex - Hill Brow, Nursted, Rake; Hants/Wilts - Bramshaw, Brook, Canada, Faberstown, Furzley, Henley, North Charford, North Tidworth, Tangley Bottom, West Dean

RECORDS

Hants/IoW records at TheGenealogist.co.uk:
- **Trade directories:** seven from 1830 to 1925.
- **Parish registers** for around 100 parishes in Hampshire and the Isle of Wight (see www.thegenealogist.co.uk/coverage/parish-records/hampshire/); plus some transcriptions of Huguenot and Catholic records.
- **Land owners:** tithe commutation records, and some tithe maps.
- **School registers** for Winchester College, 1836-1906.

SURNAMES

Common Hants and Isle of Wight names:

Hampshire 1841	Isle of Wight 1841
COOPER	YOUNG
KNIGHT	WHEELER
KING	COOPER
BAKER	MORRIS
CARTER	SALTER
COOK	SAUNDERS
HUNT	JOLLIFFE
MARTIN	JAMES
YOUNG	DYER
ROGERS	BULL
NEWMAN	BAKER

RESOURCES

- Hampshire Record Office, Winchester, www3.hants.gov.uk/archives.htm
- Isle of Wight Record Office, Newport, www.iwight.com/Residents/Libraries-Cultural-and-Heritage/Records-Office/
- Hampshire Genealogical Society, www.hgs-online.org.uk
- Isle of Wight Family History Society, www.isle-of-wight-fhs.co.uk
- Royal Hampshire Regiment Museum, Winchester, www.serleshouse.co.uk
- Find other resources at www.genuki.org.uk/big/eng/HAM/ and www.genuki.org.uk/big/eng/IOW/

The county has in the past been called Southamptonshire and the name of the administrative county was only changed from 'County of Southampton' in 1959. Although the Isle of Wight has at times been part of Hampshire, it has been administratively independent since 1890 (it had a brief period as an independent kingdom in the 15th century). The towns of Bournemouth and Christchurch also fall within the traditional county.

Hampshire was the departure point of some of those later to settle on the east coast of what is now the United States in the 17th century, giving its name in particular to the state of New Hampshire.

During the English Civil War King Charles fled to the Isle of Wight, believing he would receive sympathy from the governor, Robert Hammond. Hammond was appalled, and imprisoned the king in Carisbrooke Castle. In the Seven Years' War, the island was used as a staging post for British troops departing on expeditions against the French coast.

The isle was primarily agricultural, with some brick-making, pottery and cement industries, as well as shipbuilding at Cowes. Queen Victoria made Osborne House on the Isle of Wight her summer home for many years and, as a result, it became a major holiday resort for fashionable Victorians. ⚙

Herefordshire

Herefordshire is one of the historic counties of England, dating back to Anglo-Saxon times. More than a millennium later, it remains predominantly an agricultural region, with only one larger settlement, the cathedral city of Hereford. Only the wilds of Northumberland and Cumbria have a lower population density.

Herefordshire's rural atmosphere may not have changed a great deal, but its borders have – in early centuries its borders with Wales led to frequent changes, and their proximity means many place names have a Welsh flavour. Welsh was even spoken in many areas of the county until the 19th century. For centuries the southern and western area of the county, known as Archenfield, had uncertain status between the two countries. The 10th century Danish invasion reached as far as this area.

In more modern times, between 1974 and 1998 the whole county was absorbed into 'Hereford and Worcester'.

Herefordshire was governed by a sheriff as early as the reign of Edward the Confessor, the shire court meeting at Hereford where later the assizes and Quarter Sessions were also held. In 1606 an act was passed declaring Hereford free from the jurisdiction of the Council of Wales, but the county was not finally relieved from the interference of the Marcher Lords (appointed by the monarch to oversee the border) until the reign of William and Mary.

Herefordshire was first represented in parliament in 1295, although the

HISTORIC COUNTY BOUNDARIES

1844: Transferred to other counties: part of the township of Litton and Cascob (in the parishes of Cascob and Presteigne) to Radnorshire; the hamlet of Bwlch Trewyn (in the parish of Cwmyoy) to Monmouthshire; the chapelry of Farlow (in the parish of Stottesdon) to Shropshire; the chapelry of Rochford (in the parish of Tenbury) to Worcestershire

1844: Transferred from other counties: the township of Lea Lower (in the parish of Lea) from Gloucestershire; the parish of Welsh Bicknor from Monmouthshire

1891: The detached parish of Fwthog was transferred to Monmouthshire

Parishes across two counties: Gloucs/Herefords - Clifford's Mesne, Dancing Green, Lea Line; Herefords/Worcs - West Malvern, Wynds Point

RECORDS

Herefordshire records online at
TheGenealogist.co.uk:

- **Trade directories:** seven directories
  from 1835 to 1934.

- **Parish registers** for Bosbury,
  Coddington, Ledbury, Sarnesfield, Canon
  Frome and Munsley.

- **Land owners:** tithe commutation
  records and some maps.

- The 1936 Hereford Register of **Electors**.

SURNAMES

Common Herefordshire names:

1841	1911
PRICE	PRICE
POWELL	POWELL
LEWIS	LEWIS
WATKINS	WATKINS
MORGAN	MORGAN
DAVIS	MORRIS
PREECE	PREECE
GRIFFITHS	GRIFFITHS
MORRIS	JAMES
HILL	HARRIS

RESOURCES

- Herefordshire Archives and Record Centre, Hereford, www.herefordshire.gov.uk/archives
- Herefordshire Through Time website, http://htt.herefordshire.gov.uk
- Herefordshire Family History Society, www.herefordshirefhs.org.uk
- Herefordshire Light Infantry Museum, Hereford, www.herefordshirelightinfantrymuseum.com
- Find other resources at www.genuki.org.uk/big/eng/HEF/

boroughs made very irregular returns and from 1306 to 1627, only Hereford and Leominster were represented.

During the Wars of the Roses the influence of the Mortimers led the county to support the Yorkist cause, and Edward, afterwards Edward IV, raised 23,000 men in this neighbourhood. The Battle of Mortimer's Cross was fought in 1461 near Wigmore. Before the outbreak of the civil war of the 17th century, complaints of illegal taxation were rife in Herefordshire, but a strong anti-Puritan feeling led the county to favour the royalist cause.

Herefordshire has always been an exceptionally rich agricultural area, where manufacture has been unimportant, with the sole exception of the woollen and the cloth trade which flourished soon after the Norman conquest. Iron was worked in Wormelow hundred in Roman times, and the Domesday Survey mentions iron workers in Marcle. At the time of Henry VIII the county's towns had become much impoverished, and Elizabeth I, in order to encourage local industries, insisted on her subjects wearing English-made caps from the factory of Hereford.

Hops were grown in the county soon after their introduction into England in 1524. In 1580 and again in 1637 the county was severely visited by the plague. In the 17th century it had a flourishing timber trade, and was also noted for its orchards and cider, and remains so today. 🏴

Hertfordshire

Hertfordshire was founded in the Norse–Saxon wars of the 9th century, and developed through commerce serving London rather than agriculture. Its clay soil was not well-suited to crop cultivation with a medieval plough, although the county did grow good barley which later became important for brewing.

The Roman era saw the development of several new towns, including Verulamium (St Albans) where in c293 the first recorded British martyrdom is traditionally believed to have taken place.

By the 6th century the majority of the modern county was part of the East Saxon kingdom. This relatively short-lived kingdom collapsed in the 9th century, ceding the territory of Hertfordshire to the control of the West Anglians of Mercia. The region finally became an English shire in the 10th century.

A century later William of Normandy received the surrender of the surviving senior English lords and clergy at Berkhamsted, before being crowned at Westminster.

In the high middle ages, the county was relatively urbanised by medieval standards, but there was no large conurbation. Commerce grew in Hertfordshire from the start of the 12th century; the number of markets and fairs rose steadily from about 1100 until the Black Death. From the 13th century, the county traded in butter and cheese and, to a lesser extent, meat, hides and leather. The county also developed inns and other services for travellers to and from London.

The Knights Templar built Baldock, starting around 1140. At around

HISTORIC COUNTY BOUNDARIES

1844: Transferred to other counties: part of the hamlet of Coleshill (in the parish of Amersham) to Buckinghamshire; parts of the parishes of Meppershall and Studham in Hertfordshire transferred to Bedfordshire

1844: Transferred from other counties: part of the parish of Ickleford from Bedfordshire

Parishes across two counties: Beds/Herts - Caddington, Dunstable, Lower Green, Markyate, Pepperstock; Bucks/Herts - Chorleywood; Cambs/Herts - Royston; Herts/Middx - Barnet Gate, Cockfosters, Elstree, Hadley, Little Heath, New Barnet, New Southgate, Ridge

RECORDS

Herts records at TheGenealogist.co.uk:
- **Trade directories:** seven directories from 1862 to 1929.
- **Parish registers** for nearly 60 parishes (see www.thegenealogist.co.uk/coverage/parish-records/hertfordshire/).
- **Land owners:** tithe commutation records and maps.

SURNAMES

Common Hertfordshire names:

1841	1911
KING	CLARK
DAY	KING
GREEN	CHAPMAN
HILL	HILL
CARTER	DAY
CHAPMAN	GRAY

RESOURCES

- Hertfordshire Archives and Local Studies, Hertford, www.hertsdirect.org/hals
- Hertfordshire Family History Society, www.hertsfhs.org.uk
- Letchworth & District Family History Group, www.ldfhg.org.uk
- Royston & District FHS, www.roystonfhs.org.uk
- Stevenage Family History Society, www.stevenagefhs.webspace.virginmedia.com
- Bedfordshire & Hertfordshire Regiment Gallery, www.lutonculture.com/wardown-park-museum/galleries-and-exhibitions/hertfordshire-and-bedfordshire-regiment-gallery/
- Find other resources at www.genuki.org.uk/big/eng/HRT/

the same time, the leatherworking trade was prominent in Hitchin. Nicholas Breakspear, the only Englishman ever to have been elected Pope, was born on a farm in near Abbots Langley around 1100.

One of the first three printing presses in England was in St Albans. England's first paper mill stood in Hertford from 1494.

The 14th century Black Death massively reduced Hertfordshire's population. The subsequent economic conditions contributed to the Peasants' Revolt in 1381, which involved many Hertfordshire people. After the leader Wat Tyler had been caught and executed, Richard II went to St Albans to quell the rebels. In the 15th century, three battles in the Wars of the Roses took place in Herts, two of them at St Albans.

The 17th century saw the creation of Hugh Myddelton's New River, an artificial watercourse that predated the building of England's canal network by over a century. The Grand Junction Canal was cut across the county at the end of the 18th century.

During the 18th century brewing became an important industry in Hertfordshire. Agriculture also improved, thanks to greater mechanisation.

In 1903, Letchworth became the world's first garden city and Stevenage became the first town to redevelop under the New Towns Act 1946.

From the 1920s until the late 1980s, the town of Borehamwood was home to one of the major British film studio complexes, Elstree.

Kent

Kent, one of the 'home counties', is known as the 'Garden of England' for its rich agricultural land, especially for orchards and hop fields. Maidstone is its county town and historically Rochester and Canterbury have been cities. Major industries in the north-west of Kent have included cement, papermaking, and aircraft construction, but these are now in decline. The county also had a handful of coal mines.

East Kent became one of the kingdoms of the Jutes during the 5th century AD and the area was later known as Cantia in around 730 and Cent in 835.

Kent played an important role in the spread of Christianity, with St Augustine arriving in Thanet in 597 – he became the first Archbishop of Canterbury. During the medieval and early modern period, Kent played a major role in several of England's most notable rebellions, including the Peasants' Revolt of 1381, Jack Cade's rebellion of 1450, and Wyatt's Rebellion of 1554 against Queen Mary I.

England has relied on the county's ports to provide warships through much of the past 800 years; the Cinque Ports in the 12th–14th centuries and Chatham Dockyard in the 16th–20th centuries were of particular importance to the country's security. By the 17th century, tensions between Britain and the continental powers of the Netherlands and France led to increasing military build-up in the county. Forts were built all along the coast following a daring raid by the Dutch navy on the shipyards of the Medway towns in 1667. The 18th century was dominated by wars with France, during which the Medway became the primary base for a fleet that could act along

HISTORIC COUNTY BOUNDARIES

1889:   The County of London was created and the townships of Deptford, Greenwich, Woolwich, Lee, Eltham, Charlton, Kidbrooke and Lewisham were transferred out of Kent

1900:   The area of Penge was gained

1965:   The London boroughs of Bromley and Bexley were created from nine towns formerly in Kent

Parishes across two counties: Kent/Surrey - Anerley, Honor Oak, Nunhead, Penge, Spring Park; Kent/Sussex - Lamberhurst

RECORDS

Kent records at TheGenealogist.co.uk:
- **Trade directories:** nine directories from 1839 to 1938.
- **Parish registers** for around 30 parishes (see www.thegenealogist.co.uk/coverage/parish-records/kent/).
- **Land owners:** tithe commutation records.
- **School registers** for Dover College, 1871-1924, King's School, Canterbury, 1859-1931, and Tonbridge School, 1826-1910.
- **Regimental records** of the West Kent (Queen's Own) Yeomanry 1794-1909.
- Maidstone **electors** and an 1832 poll book.
- Some **wills** and 17th century **visitations**.

SURNAMES

Common XXX names:

1841	1911
BAKER	BAKER
MARTIN	MARTIN
CHAPMAN	KING
KING	HARRIS
CLARK	CLARK
MARSH	TURNER
HARRIS	CHAPMAN
RUSSELL	COLLINS
YOUNG	MARSH
TURNER	RUSSELL
HILLS	COOPER
DAVIS	

RESOURCES

- Kent History & Library Centre, Maidstone, www.kent.gov.uk/leisure-and-community/history-and-heritage/kent-history-and-library-centre
- Folkestone & District Family History Society, www.folkfhs.org.uk
- North West Kent FHS, www.nwkfhs.org.uk
- Tunbridge Wells FHS, www.tunwells-fhs.co.uk
- Woolwich & District FHS, www.woolwichfhs.org.uk
- Queen's Own Royal West Kent Regiment Museum, Maidstone, www.museum.maidstone.gov.uk/queensown/
- The Buffs (Royal East Kent Regiment) Museum, Canterbury, www.canterbury.co.uk/Beaney/collections/The-Buffs.aspx
- Find other resources at www.genuki.org.uk/big/eng/KEN/

the Dutch and French coasts. Kent's location later meant that it was at the front line of the Battle of Britain during World War Two. East Kent was known as 'Hell Fire Corner' during the conflict.

In the early 19th century, smugglers were very active on the Kent coastline. Gangs brought spirits, tobacco and salt to the county, and transported goods such as wool across the sea to France.

Census data shows that Kent was not strongly affected by industrial expansion in the 19th century. In both the 1841 and 1901 censuses, the county's occupations are dominated by agricultural labourers, but the prominence of fishermen is notably absent in 1901, matching the decline in that industry. Many soldiers were listed in 1841, suggesting perhaps the county's role in national defence.

Traditionally those hailing from west of the River Medway are 'Kentish Men', and those east of there 'Men of Kent'. 🗙

Lancashire

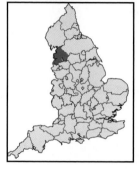

Lancashire – sometimes known as the County of Lancaster – was founded in the 12th century. In the Domesday Book of 1086, some of its lands were treated as part of Yorkshire. The land that lay between the Ribble and Mersey, *inter Ripam et Mersam*, was included in the returns for Cheshire. When its boundaries were established, it bordered Cumberland, Westmorland, Yorkshire and Cheshire.

During the Industrial Revolution it emerged from being a sparsely populated agricultural area as a major commercial and industrial region. The county encompassed several hundred mill towns and collieries.

By the 1830s, approximately 85% of all cotton manufactured worldwide was processed in Lancashire. Preston, Accrington, Blackburn, Bolton, Rochdale, Oldham, Chorley, Darwen, Nelson, Colne, Burnley and Wigan were major cotton mill towns during this time. Blackpool was a major centre for tourism for the inhabitants of Lancashire's mill towns, particularly during 'wakes week' in the summer.

In the 19th century, mining was another important part of the county's industry, though on the coast there was also fishing. Historically, the docks in Preston formed an industrial port.

Lancashire was also historically the location of the port of Liverpool, while Barrow-in-Furness (now in Cumbria) is famous for shipbuilding.

Census data confirms the importance of the textile trade. In 1841, the

HISTORIC COUNTY BOUNDARIES

1972: the Furness exclave (North Lonsdale) of Lancashire and Cartmel were fused into the new county of Cumbria. Liverpool and Manchester with most of their surrounding conurbations were removed to form part of the metropolitan counties of Merseyside and Greater Manchester respectively. Warrington and surrounding districts including the villages of Winwick, Croft, Risley and Culcheth were annexed to Cheshire. A part of the West Riding of Yorkshire near Clitheroe, was transferred to Lancashire.

Parishes across three boundaries: Cheshire/Lancs/Yorkshire – Mossley

RECORDS

Lancashire records at TheGenealogist.co.uk:
- **Trade directories:** 12 from 1772 to 1937.
- **Parish registers:** see www.thegenealogist.co.uk/coverage/parish-records/Lancashire/); plus some Catholic registers.
- **Land owners:** tithe commutation records and some maps.
- **School registers:** for Manchester School (1730-1837) and Rossall School (1844-1882).
- **Regimental records:** The 42nd (East Lancashire) Division; The King's Own (Royal Lancaster Regiment); Manchester City Battalions; 55th (West Lancashire) Division.
- 16th/17th century medieval **visitations**.
- Numerous **wills** from 1301 to 1812.

SURNAMES

Common Lancashire names:

1841	1911
JACKSON	JACKSON
HARRISON	HARRISON
WALKER	THOMPSON
ASHWORTH	HUGHES
HOLT	WALKER
TURNER	SHAW
HUGHES	GREEN
THOMPSON	
HOWARTH	

RESOURCES

- Lancashire Archives, Preston, www.lancashire.gov.uk/libraries-and-archives/archives-and-record-office.aspx
- Liverpool Record Office, https://liverpool.gov.uk/libraries/archives-family-history
- Manchester Record Office, www.manchester.gov.uk/info/448/archives_and_local_history
- Lancashire Family History & Heraldry Society, www.lfhhs.org
- Manchester & Lancashire Family History Society, www.mlfhs.org.uk
- Lancashire Infantry Museum, www.lancashireinfantrymuseum.org.uk
- Find other resources at www.genuki.org.uk/big/eng/LAN/

top 20 professions included weaver, spinner, tailer and dressmaker – although mining and agriculture also feature.

The Liverpool and Manchester Railway opened in 1830 and was the first railway in the world to rely exclusively on steam power, with no horse-drawn traffic permitted at any time.

It was also the first railway be entirely double track throughout its length; the first to have a signalling system; the first to be fully timetabled; the first to be powered entirely by its own motive power; and the first to carry mail.

By 1911, when the population had soared to 4.8 million from 1.7 million 70 years earlier, agriculture has faded but textiles and mining remain key professions, despite their decline by this time in other parts of the country. Dock labourer was another trade in the top 20, highlighting the importance of Liverpool in particular in connecting the nation to the world. ✠

Leicestershire

Three first recorded use of the name Leicestershire was in the 11th century. Its boundaries have changed little since the Domesday Survey. In the 7th century, the region formed part of the kingdom of Mercia. In the 9th century the district was subjugated by the Vikings, and Leicester became one of the five Danish boroughs.

Among the earliest historical events connected with the county were the siege and capture of Leicester by Henry II in 1173 after the rebellion of the Earl of Leicester. Parliament was held at Leicester in 1414.

During the Wars of the Roses Leicester was a great Lancastrian stronghold. In 1485 the battle of Bosworth was fought in the county. In the Civil War of the 17th century, the greater part of the county favoured parliament, though the mayor and some members of the corporation of Leicester sided with the king. In 1645 Leicester was twice captured by the Royalist forces.

The county has a long history of agriculture, particulary dairy farming. The woollen industry flourished in Leicestershire in Norman times, and in 1343 Leicestershire wool was rated at a higher value than that of most other counties. Coal was worked at Coleorton in the early 15th century and at Measham in the 17th century. The modern Snibston Discovery Park is built on one of three coal mines that operated in Coalville from the 1820s until 1986. Blue slate has been quarried at Swithland for centuries, and a limestone quarry at Barrow-on-Soar is also very ancient.

The staple manufacture of the county historically, hosiery, originated in the 17th century, the chief centres being Leicester, Hinckley and Loughbor-

HISTORIC COUNTY BOUNDARIES

1884: Packington gained from Derbyshire

1897: Appleby Magna North, Chilcote, Measham, Oakthorpe, Stretton en le Field, Willesley gained from Derbyshire

1897: Netherseal and Overseal moved to Derbyshire

Parishes across two counties: Derbys/Leics – Appleby Magna, Boundary, Donisthorpe, Short Heath, Woodville; Leics/Lincs – Sewstern; Leics/Northants – Market Harborough Leics/Warks – No Man's Heath

RECORDS

Leics records at TheGenealogist.co.uk:
- **Trade directories:** nine directories from 1835 to 1941.
- **Parish registers** for more than 80 parishes (see www.thegenealogist.co.uk/coverage/parish-records/leicestershire/).
- **Land owners:** tithe commutation records and maps.
- **Freemen** of Leicester from 1196 to 1930.
- Indexes of **wills** from 1495 and 1660.
- 1619 medieval **visitations**.

SURNAMES

Common Leicestershire names:

1841	1911
WARD	CLARKE
CLARKE	MOORE
COOPER	WARD
HILL	HILL
MOORE	ALLEN
GREEN	COOPER
ALLEN	HARRIS
BAILEY	BAILEY
KING	

RESOURCES

- Leicestershire Record Office, Wigston, www.leics.gov.uk/recordoffice
- Leicestershire & Rutland Family History Society, www.lrfhs.org.uk
- Museum of the Royal Leicestershire Regiment, Leicester, www.royalleicestershireregiment.org.uk/the-regimental-museum
- Find other resources at www.genuki.org.uk/big/eng/LEI/

ough. Before the development of steam-driven frames in the 19th century, hand framework-knitting of hose and gloves was carried on in about a hundred villages. Wool-carding was also an extensive industry before 1840.

Other industries in the county have included the manufacture of boots and shoes in Market Harborough, plus brickmaking and iron founding. Melton Mowbray gives its name to a well-known manufacture of pork pies, and since the mid-18th century, Stilton cheese has been made near there.

Leicestershire is considered to be the birthplace of fox hunting as it is known today. Hugo Meynell, who lived in Quorn in the 18th century, is known as the father of modern fox hunting. Melton Mowbray and Market Harborough have particular associations with the sport.

Engineering has long been an important part of the economy of Leicestershire. John Taylor Bellfounders continues a history of bellfounding in Loughborough since the 14th century. In 1881 John Taylor cast the largest bell in Britain, 'Great Paul', for St Paul's Cathedral in London. Meanwhile Norman & Underwood has been making sand-cast sheet lead roofing and stained glass since 1825, working on many of England's major cathedrals and historic buildings.

Abbey Pumping Station houses four enormous steam powered beam engines built in Leicester in the 1890s in the Vulcan factory owned by Josiah Gimson. 🎖

Lincolnshire

Lincolnshire originally derived from the merging of the territory of the ancient Kingdom of Lindsey with that controlled by the Danelaw borough of Stamford. For some time the entire county was called 'Lindsey', and it is recorded as such in the Domesday Book. Later, Lindsey was applied only the northern area, around Lincoln, and emerged as one of the three 'Parts of Lincolnshire', along with the Parts of Holland in the south east and Kesteven in the south west.

The Romans had a strong presence in the county but, after they left in the fifth century, their many works gradually fell into ruin and disrepair. Incoming groups of Angles settled heavily in the northern part of the county, which was later raided by the Vikings in the 9th century. Scandinavian settlers followed the raiders and left their legacy in many Lincolnshire place names.

In the Middle Ages the Witham valley between Boston and Lincoln had the highest concentration of abbeys and monastic foundations in the country. Conversely the county had surprisingly few castles.

Fairs at Stamford, Grantham, and Stow Fair were established, and lasted throughout the period. Corby Glen sheep fair has been held more or less unchanged every year since 1238.

Sheep farming and the wool trade brought new wealth to the area, and underwrote the building of many fine churches. An important medieval book, the Luttrell Psalter, forms the basis for nearly every schoolbook illustration of the period. It lay unregarded in the church at Irnham until the early 20th century, when it was saved for the nation.

During the Protestant reformation, Lincolnshire had strong pro-Catholic sentiments, and on 2 October 1536 an anti-Anglican peasant rebellion broke out. The leaders of this rebellion were local peasants and

HISTORIC COUNTY BOUNDARIES

1888: the northern part of the county, with Scunthorpe and Grimsby, went to the newly formed Humberside (abolished in 1996).

Parishes across two counties: Cambs/Lincs - Tydd Gote; Leics/Lincs - Sewstern; Lincs/Yorks - Eastoft, Garthorpe, Fockerby

RECORDS

Lincs records at TheGenealogist.co.uk:
- **Trade directories:** five directories from 1850 to 1933.
- **Parish registers** for more than 80 parishes (see www.thegenealogist.co.uk/coverage/parish-records/lincolnshire/).
- **Land owners:** tithe commutation records and some maps.
- **Wills:** a collection of Lincoln wills from 1540 to 1659.
- **Visitation records** for 1666, and a compilation of Lincolnshire Domesday Book records.

SURNAMES

Common Lincolnshire names:

1841	1911
JACKSON	CLARK
CLARK	JACKSON
HARRISON	GREEN
THOMPSON	THOMPSON
GREEN	COOK
MARS	WARD
COOK	HARRISON
PARKER	PARKER
RICHARDSON	WALKER
WALKER	MARS
CHAPMAN	HILL

RESOURCES

- Lincolnshire Record Office, Lincoln, www.lincolnshire.gov.uk/visiting/lincolnshire-archives/
- Lincolnshire Family History Society, www.lincolnshirefhs.org.uk
- Isle of Axholme FHS, www.axholme-fhs.org.uk
- The Royal Lincolnshire Regiment Museum, Lincoln, www.thelincolnshireregiment.org/museum.shtml
- Find other resources at www.genuki.org.uk/big/eng/LIN/

Catholic priests. King Henry VIII responded by dispatching an army of 3,000 soldiers to quell the rebellion.

During the English Civil War, Lincolnshire was part of the Eastern Association, the Parliamentarian alliance. On its western border lay the Royalist strongholds of Newark on Trent and Belvoir Castle. Lincolnshire was therefore raided and defended by both sides.

Lincolnshire has been predominantly agricultural throughout its history, and remains so. In the late 1930s, despite its coastal holiday industry, fishing industries, iron mining and smelting and heavy machinery manufacturing, Lincolnshire was large enough to give an impression of being a largely unvisited, peaceful agricultural backwater.

In World War Two, its size, gentle topography and relative proximity to the enemy led to a rapid expansion in the number of Royal Air Force bases in the county. By 1945 there were 46 of them.

Lincolnshire still has the strongest claim to being the home of RAF Bomber Command, playing host to many squadrons, including the Lancaster bombers of the famous 617 Dambusters squadron, who were based at RAF Scampton. ✠

London & Middlesex

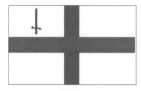

London has always been a city of renewal – plagues and fires have decimated its population and scarred its buildings, but every time it has recovered and rebuilt itself bigger and better than before. Little wonder, then, that so many of our ancestors were drawn there, whether from dwindling rural settlements around the country or from countries across the globe.

Of course, for many of them the dream of new opportunities turned into a nightmare of slum life in the insanitary and crime-ridden 'rookeries'. But the ever-changing city also brought with it employment in trades from cab driving to lamplighting, from being a Thames lighterman (working on barges) to a bookbinder in Clerkenwell.

London's expansion beyond the boundaries of the City really began in the 17th century. Immediately to the north was Moorfields, which had recently been drained and laid out in walks, but it was frequented by beggars – travellers, who crossed it in order to get into London, tried not to linger. Mile End, then a common on the Great Eastern Road, was known as a rendezvous for troops. The general meeting-place of Londoners in the daytime was the nave of Old St Paul's Cathedral. Merchants conducted business in the aisles, and used the font as a counter upon which to make their payments; lawyers received clients at their particular pillars; and the unemployed looked for work.

St Paul's Churchyard was the centre of the book trade and Fleet Street

---

HISTORIC COUNTY BOUNDARIES

1889: When the County of London was formed in 1889, it was made up of a number of parishes in Kent, Surrey and Middlesex. One parish in the latter, Clerkenwell, had a detached part (Alexandra Park) that became an exclave of London surrounded by Middlesex. This was absorbed by Middlesex in 1899

1889: The whole of South Hornsey, including detached parts of Middlesex, passed to the County of London

1965: The administrative county of Greater London was formally created, replacing the administrative counties of Middlesex and London, and absorbing parts of Essex, Hertfordshire, Kent and Surrey

Parishes across two counties: Herts/Middx – Barnet Gate, Cockfosters, Elstree, Hadley, Little Heath, New Barnet, New Southgate, Ridge

RECORDS

London and Middlesex records at TheGenealogist.co.uk:
- **Trade directories:** around 70 directories for London and a further 3 for Middlesex.
- **Parish registers** for more than 40 London parishes and more than 30 in Middlesex (see www.thegenealogist.co.uk/coverage/parish-records/.
- **Land owners:** tithe commutation records and maps for Middlesex.
- **School/college registers** for Blackheath High School, City and Guilds College, London School of Economics and Political Science, Royal Holloway College, Mill Hill School, St Pauls School, University College School, Harrow School and Merchant Taylor's School; plus a register of admissions for Grays Inn.
- Records of the Middlesex **yeomanry**.
- Westminster **poll books** from 1774, 1818 and 1841.
- London **wills** from 1258 to 1688.
- Medieval **visitations** from 1568 and 1633.

SURNAMES

Common London names:

1841	1911
DAVIS	HARRIS
GREEN	CLARK
WOOD	KING
KING	DAVIS
BAKER	GREEN
HARRIS	BAKER
COOPER	MARTIN
TURNER	TURNER

Common Middlesex names:

1841	1911
CLARK	CLARK
KING	KING
GREEN	HARRIS
HARRIS	BAKER
CARTER	TURNER
WEBB	HILL
HILL	MARTIN
COOPER	COOPER

RESOURCES

- London Metropolitan Archives, www.cityoflondon.gov.uk/things-to-do/london-metropolitan-archives
- London Westminster & Middlesex Family History Society, www.lwmfhs.org.uk
- West Middlesex FHS, www.west-middlesex-fhs.org.uk
- East of London FHS, www.eolfhs.org.uk
- National Army Museum, www.nam.ac.uk
- Find other resources at www.genuki.org.uk/big/eng/LND and www.genuki.org.uk/big/eng/MDX

was a centre of public entertainment. During Charles I's unpopular reign, aristocrats began to inhabit the West End in large numbers. Country landowners and their families lived in London for part of the year simply for the social life – the 'London season'.

Overcrowding saw plagues throughout the centuries. As James I was about to take the throne in 1603, a plague killed around 30,000 people, and the Great Plague of 1665 killed more than twice that – a fifth of the population. Diarist Samuel Pepys, most famous for describing the Great Fire in the following year, wrote that 6000 people died in one week and

London & Middlesex (continued)

there was "little noise heard day or night but tolling of bells".

Although the fire saw little loss of life, it ultimately changed London from a medieval city to a modern one. Many aristocratic residents never returned to the City itself, preferring to take new houses in the West End, where fashionable new districts such as St James's were built close to the main royal residence of Whitehall Palace. The rural lane of Piccadilly sprouted courtiers' mansions such as Burlington House. The separation between the middle class mercantile City of London, and the aristocratic world of the court in Westminster became complete.

The East End also became heavily populated in the decades after the Great Fire. London's docks began to extend downstream, attracting many working people who worked on the docks themselves and in the processing and distributive trades. These people lived in Whitechapel, Wapping, Stepney and Limehouse, generally in slum conditions. Meanwhile the Revocation of the Edict of Nantes in 1685 led to a large migration of Huguenots to London, typically working as silk weavers in Spitalfields.

London began to become the hub of the future empire as the 18th century began. The Bank of England was founded, and the British East India Company was expanding its influence. Lloyd's of London also began to operate. In 1700 London handled 80% of England's imports and 69% of its exports. This role as a trading post meant that London never relied on industry in the same way as the great cities of the North and Midlands. As people flocked to London to trade and seek employment, crime grew in proportion. The Bow Street Runners were established in 1750 as a professional police force. Penalties for crime were harsh, with the death penalty being applied for fairly minor crimes. Public hangings were common in London, and were popular public events.

In 1780 London was rocked by the Gordon Riots, an uprising by Protestants against Roman Catholic emancipation led by Lord George Gordon. Severe damage was caused to Catholic churches and homes, and 285 rioters were killed.

A more peaceful phenomenon of 18th century London was the coffee house, which became a popular place to debate ideas. Growing literacy and the development of the printing press meant that news became widely available. Fleet Street became the centre of the embryonic British press.

During the 19th century, London was transformed into the world's largest city and capital of the British Empire. Its population expanded from 1 million in 1800 to 6.7 million a century later. While the city grew wealthy as Britain's holdings expanded, 19th century London was also a city of poverty, where millions lived in overcrowded and unsanitary slums, as immortalised by Dickens.

Famous 'rookeries' include the St Giles area of central London, which existed from the 17th century and into Victorian times. It was demolished in the late 19th century along with others in the East End as part of slum clearance and urban redevelopment projects.

London's next major transformation came with the railways, above and then below ground. These allowed the development of suburbs in neighboring counties from which middle-class and wealthy people could commute to the centre. The growth of greater London again exacerbated the class divide, with the poor left to inhabit the inner city areas.

As the capital of a massive empire, London saw ever more waves of immigrants from the colonies and poorer parts of Europe. A large Irish population settled in the city during the Victorian period, at one point making up about 20% of London's population. London also became home to a sizeable Jewish community, and small communities of Chinese and South Asians settled in the city. To this day London retains its rich and diverse character, making London ancestry exciting to explore. ✠

MIDDLESEX

Middlesex is now mostly part of Greater London, but was first established as the Anglo-Saxon territory of the Middle Saxons (before that it was part of the Kingdom of Essex). The historic county included land stretching north of the River Thames and the rivers Colne and Lea as other boundaries. The City of London was a county in its own right from the 12th century and exerted political control over Middlesex, with Westminster Abbey dominating its financial, judicial and ecclesiastical aspects.

The economy of the county was dependent on the City of London from early times and was primarily agricultural. A variety of goods were provided for the City, including crops such as grain and hay, livestock and building materials. Recreation at day trip destinations such as Hackney, Islington, Highgate and Twickenham, as well as coaching, inn-keeping and sale of goods and services at shops and stalls to the considerable passing trade provided much local employment and also formed part of the early economy. However, during the 18th century the inner parishes of Middlesex became suburbs of the City and were increasingly urbanised.

The introduction of radial railway lines from 1839 caused a fundamental shift away from agricultural supply for London towards large-scale house building. Tottenham, Edmonton and Enfield in the north developed first as working-class residential suburbs with easy access to central London.

Norfolk

Norfolk was settled in pre-Roman times. The Iceni tribe inhabited the county from the 1st century BC to the end of the 1st century AD. The Iceni revolted against the Roman invasion in 47 AD, and again in 60 AD led by Boudica. The crushing of the second rebellion opened the county to the Romans. During the Roman era roads and ports were constructed throughout the county.

Norfolk was vulnerable to invasion from Scandinavia and Northern Europe, and forts were built to defend against the Angles and Saxons. By the 5th century the Angles had established control of the region and later became the 'north folk' and the 'south folk', hence Norfolk and Suffolk. These became part of the kingdom of East Anglia, which later merged with Mercia and then Wessex.

In the 9th century the region again came under attack, this time from Danes who killed the king, Edmund the Martyr. In the centuries before the Norman conquest the wetlands of the east of the county began to be converted to farmland, and settlements grew in these areas. Migration into East Anglia must have been high as by the time of the Conquest and Domesday Book survey it was one of the most densely populated parts of the British Isles.

During the Middle Ages the county developed arable agriculture and woollen industries. Norfolk's prosperity at that time is evident from its large number of mediaeval churches: of an original total of over a thousand, 659 survive, more than in the whole of the rest of Great Britain. The economy was in decline by the time of the Black Death, which dramatically reduced the population in 1349. Over a third of the population of Norwich died during a plague epidemic in 1579. By the 16th century Norwich had grown to become the second largest city in England, but in 1665 the Great Plague again killed around a third of the population.

During the English Civil War Norfolk was largely Parliamentarian. The economy and agriculture of the region declined somewhat. During the

HISTORIC COUNTY BOUNDARIES

Parishes across two counties: Cambs/Norfolk - Emneth, Holly End, Outwell, Upwell, Welney, Wisbech; Norfolk/Suffolk - Brandon, Rushford, Thetford

RECORDS

Norfolk records at TheGenealogist.co.uk:
- **Trade directories:** four directories from 1858 to 1937.
- **Parish registers** for more than 100 parishes (see www.thegenealogist.co.uk/coverage/parish-records/norfolk/).
- **Land owners:** tithe commutation records.
- **Freemen** of Norwich from 1317-1603.
- **Poll books** for 1768, 1806, 1817, 1865.
- **Visitations** from 1563, 1589, 1613, 1664.

SURNAMES

Common Norfolk names:

1841	1911
GREEN	CLARKE
CLARKE	MOORE
MOORE	COOPER
COOPER	HOWARD
WARD	KING
HOWARD	WARD
CHAPMAN	PALMER
KING	ALLEN
PALMER	CHAPMAN
TURNER	TURNER

RESOURCES

- Norfolk Record Office, Norwich, www.archives.norfolk.gov.uk
- Norfolk Family History Society, www.norfolkfhs.org.uk
- Mid Norfolk FHS, www.tsites.co.uk/sites/mnfhs/
- Royal Norfolk Regimental Museum, www.royalnorfolkregimentalmuseum.org.uk
- Find other resources at www.genuki.org.uk/big/eng/NFK/

Industrial Revolution Norfolk developed little industry, except in Norwich, and was a late addition to the railway network.

Norwich has traditionally been the home of various dissident minorities, notably the French Huguenot and the Belgian Walloon communities in the 16th and 17th centuries, who numbered as many as a third of the population. Many of them worked as weavers. Another important trade in the city was shoemaking.

Britain's first provincial newspaper, the *Norwich Post*, was published in 1701. In the mid-18th century some parishes listed three quarters of the men as literate. In the 1780s Norwich shawls became an important industry, although by the 1790s the wool trade began declining from competition and the loss of international markets. In 1797 Thomas Bignold, a 36-year-old wine merchant and banker, founded the first Norwich Union Society to provide insurance.

In the 20th century the county found a role in aviation. The first development in airfields came with World War One; there was then a massive expansion during World War Two with the growth of the Royal Air Force and the influx of the American USAAF 8th Air Force which operated from many Norfolk airfields. During and after World War Two, agriculture in the county rapidly intensified. ✠

Northamptonshire

In the 1st century BC, most of what later became Northamptonshire became part of the territory of the Catuvellauni, a Belgic tribe, conquered in turn by the Romans in 43 AD. The Roman road of Watling Street passed through the county, and an important Roman settlement, Lactodorum, stood on the site of modern-day Towcester. After the Romans left, the area eventually became part of the Anglo-Saxon kingdom of Mercia, and Northampton functioned as an administrative centre. From about 889 the area was conquered by the Danes, until being recaptured by the English under the Wessex king Edward the Elder in 917. Northamptonshire was conquered again in 940, this time by the Vikings of York.

In 1460, during the Wars of the Roses, the Battle of Northampton took place and King Henry VI was captured. The now-ruined Fotheringhay Castle was used to imprison Mary, Queen of Scots, before her execution.

George Washington, the first President of the United States of America, was born into the Washington family who had migrated to America from Northamptonshire in 1656. George Washington's great-x5-grandfather, Lawrence Washington, was Mayor of Northampton on several occasions.

During the English Civil War, Northamptonshire strongly supported the Parliamentarian cause, and the Royalist forces suffered a crushing defeat at the Battle of Naseby in 1645 in the north of the county. King Charles I was imprisoned at Holdenby House in 1647.

In the 18th and 19th centuries, parts of Northamptonshire and the surrounding area became industrialised. The local specialisation was already shoemaking and the leather industry. Northamptonshire made boots for Oliver Cromwell's New Model Army, and the making of army

HISTORIC COUNTY BOUNDARIES

1844: Transferred to other counties: part of the parish of Farndish to Bedfordshire
1844: Transferred from other counties: part of the extra-parochial place of Luffield Abbey from Buckinghamshire
Parishes across two counties: Beds/Northants - Newton Bromswold; Leics/Northants - Market Harborough

RECORDS

Northants records at TheGenealogist.co.uk:
- **Trade directories:** three directories from 1850 to 1898.
- **Parish registers** for nearly 20 parishes (see www.thegenealogist.co.uk/coverage/parish-records/northamptonshire/).
- **Land owners:** tithe commutation records and some maps.
- **Poll books** for 1702-1831.
- A calendar of **wills** 1510-1652.
- Medieval **visitations** 1564 and 1618-19.

SURNAMES

Common Northamptonshire names:

1841	1911
GREEN	CLARKE
WARD	WARD
ADAMS	ALLEN
CLARKE	HARRIS
COX	CHAPMAN
CHAPMAN	COX
WEBB	KNIGHT
DUNKLEY	ADAMS
ALLEN	BAILEY

RESOURCES

- Northamptonshire Record Office, Northampton, www.northamptonshire.gov.uk/heritage
- Northamptonshire Family History Society, www.northants-fhs.org
- Peterborough & District FHS, www.peterborofhs.org.uk
- Northamptonshire Regiment and Northamptonshire Yeomanry Collections, Abington Park, Northampton, www.northampton.gov.uk/museums
- Find other resources at www.genuki.org.uk/big/eng/NTH/

boots continued to be an important feature of the economy until the 20th century, as well as boots and shoes of other kinds. By the end of the 19th century it was probably the boot- and shoe-making capital of the world.

In the 17th century the weaving industry declined in the Northampton area, but flourished around Kettering. Other early industries were charcoal-burning, brick and tile manufacture and brewing. The industries of whip-making, pipe-making, silk-weaving and paper-making were introduced in the 17th and 18th centuries.

The iron-mines and stone-quarries of Northamptonshire were worked in Roman times, but the former were entirely neglected from the Plantagenet period until their rediscovery in 1850, while the two most famous quarries, those of Barnack and Stanion, were exhausted in the 16th century. During the 1930s, the town of Corby was established as a major centre of the steel industry. Much of Northamptonshire nevertheless remains largely rural.

The Soke of Peterborough was historically associated with and considered part of Northamptonshire. However, Peterborough had its own Quarter Sessions and, later, county council, and in 1965 it was merged with the neighbouring county of Huntingdonshire; in 1972 the city became a district of Cambridgeshire. 🕱

Northumberland

Today Northumberland is the most sparsely populated county in England. As evidence of its violent history of conflict between Scotland and England, Northumberland has more castles than any other county in England.

The region of present-day Northumberland once formed the core of the Anglian kingdom of Bernicia (from c547), which united with Deira (south of the River Tees) to form the kingdom of Northumbria in the 7th century. Northumberland is often called the 'cradle of Christianity' in England, because Christianity flourished on Lindisfarne – a tidal island north of Bamburgh, also called Holy Island – from the 7th century onwards.

Bamburgh is the historic capital of Northumberland, the 'royal' castle from before the unification of the Kingdoms of England under the monarchs of the House of Wessex in the 10th century. The Earldom of Northumberland was briefly held by the Scottish royal family but Scotland relinquished all claims to the region as part of the Treaty of York (1237).

The county of Northumberland included Newcastle upon Tyne until 1400, when the city became a county of itself. Northumberland expanded greatly in the Tudor period, annexing Berwick-upon-Tweed in 1482, Tynedale in 1495, Tynemouth in 1536, Redesdale around 1542 and Hexhamshire in 1572.

Northumberland has a history of revolt and rebellion against the government, as seen in the Rising of the North (1569-1570) against Elizabeth I. These revolts were usually led by the Earls of Northumberland, the Percy family.

The county was a focus of Jacobite support after the Restoration of

HISTORIC COUNTY BOUNDARIES

1844: Transferred from other counties: Islandshire (consisting of the chapelry of Ancroft, part of the parish of Belford, the township of Holy Island, the chapelry of Kyloe, the extra-parochial place of Monks House and the chapelry of Tweedmouth), Bedlington-shire (the parish of Bedlington), Norhamshire (the parish of Norham) and the extra parochial Farne Islands all transferred from County Durham

RECORDS

Northumberland records at TheGenealogist.co.uk:

- **Trade directories:** 10 directories from 1834 to 1938.
- **Parish registers** for nearly 20 parishes (see www.thegenealogist.co.uk/coverage/parish-records/northumberland/).
- **Land owners:** tithe commutation records.
- **School registers** for The Duke's School, Alnwick.
- **Freemen** of Newcastle-upon-Tyne from 1409-1710 and 1733-1760.
- **Poll books** from 1774 and 1841.

SURNAMES

Common Northumberland names:

1841	1911
ROBSON	ROBSON
THOMPSON	BELL
BELL	SCOTT
SCOTT	ARMSTRONG
WATSON	WATSON
ARMSTRONG	DIXON
YOUNG	RICHARDSON
DAVISON	ANDERSON
DIXON	HENDERSON
RICHARDSON	YOUNG
CHARLTON	GRAHAM
FORSTER	DAVISON
HENDERSON	

RESOURCES

- Northumberland Archives, Ashington (with a branch in Berwick-upon-Tweed), www.experiencewoodhorn.com/collections
- Northumberland & Durham Family History Society, www.ndfhs.org.uk
- Fusiliers Museum of Northumberland, Alnwick, www.northumberlandfusiliers.org.uk
- Find other resources at www.genuki.org.uk/big/eng/NBL/

1660. It was long a wild county, where outlaws and Border Reivers hid from the law. However, the frequent cross-border skirmishes and accompanying local lawlessness largely subsided after the Union of the Crowns of Scotland and England under King James I and VI in 1603.

Northumberland played a key role in the Industrial Revolution from the 18th century onwards. Many coal mines operated in the county from Tudor times onward, and there is evidence of coal working dating back to Roman times. From the 13th century, Newcastle acquired the monopoly of the river shipping and coal trade. Lead was also exported from Newcastle in the 12th century, probably from Hexhamshire. In the 13th century the salt industry flourished at the mouth of the river Blyth, and in the 15th century formed the principal occupation of the inhabitants of North and South Shields.

The region's coalfields fuelled industrial expansion in other areas of Britain, and the need to transport the coal from the collieries to the Tyne led to the development of the first railways. Shipbuilding and armaments manufacture were other important industries before the deindustrialisation of the 1980s.

Nottinghamshire

Nottinghamshire lies on the Roman Fosse Way, and there are Roman settlements in the county, for example at Mansfield and the fort at Bilborough. The county was settled by Angles around the 5th century, and became part of the kingdom of Mercia. The county's name first occurs in 1016, when the shire was harried by Canute, but until 1568 the county was administratively united with Derbyshire, under a single Sheriff. The boundaries have remained practically unaltered since the time of the Domesday survey.

Nottinghamshire was originally included in the diocese and province of York, and in 1291 formed an archdeaconry, comprising the deaneries of Nottingham, Newark, Bingham and Retford. By act of Parliament of 1836 the county was transferred to the diocese of Lincoln and province of Canterbury, with the additional deanery of Southwell. In 1884 most of the county was transferred to the newly created diocese of Southwell.

The Peverel Court, founded before 1113 for the recovery of small debts, had jurisdiction over 127 towns in Nottinghamshire, and was held at Nottingham until 1321, in 1330 at Algarthorpe and in 1790 at Lenton, being finally abolished in 1849.

The political history of Nottinghamshire centres round the town and castle of Nottingham, which was seized by Robert of Gloucester on behalf of Maud in 1140; captured by John in 1191; surrendered to Henry III by the rebellious barons in 1264; and formed an important station of Edward III in the Scottish wars. In the Wars of the Roses, the county as a whole favored the Yorkist cause, Nottingham being one of the most useful bases of Edward IV.

In the Civil War of the 17th century, most of the nobility and gentry favored the Royalist cause, but Nottingham Castle was garrisoned for Parliament, and in 1651 was ordered to be demolished.

Among the earliest industries of Nottinghamshire were the malting

HISTORIC COUNTY BOUNDARIES

Parishes across two counties: Derbys/Notts - Ilkeston, Pleasley Vale; Notts/Yorks - Bawtry

RECORDS

Notts records at TheGenealogist.co.uk:
- **Trade directories:** seven directories from 1850 to 1956.
- **Parish registers** for more than 100 parishes (see www.thegenealogist.co.uk/coverage/parish-records/nottinghamshire/).
- **Land owners:** tithe commutation records and some maps.
- Some **Domesday** records.
- **Military records** for the Sherwood Foresters (Nottinghamshire and Derbyshire Regiment)

SURNAMES

Common Nottinghamshire names:

1841	1911
WALKER	CLARKE
JACKSON	WARD
WARD	SHAW
MARS	JACKSON
SHAW	HARRISON
TURNER	MARS
GREEN	COOPER
COOPER	HOLMES
HARRISON	

RESOURCES

- Nottinghamshire Archives, Nottingham, www.nottinghamshire.gov.uk/archives
- Nottinghamshire Family History Society, www.nottsfhs.org.uk
- Sherwood Foresters (Nottinghamshire and Derbyshire Regiment) Gallery, Nottingham www.wfrmuseum.org.uk/sf_museum.htm
- Queens Royal Lancers & Nottinghamshire Yeomanry Museum, Newark, www.qrlnymuseum.co.uk
- Find other resources at www.genuki.org.uk/big/eng/NTT/

and woollen industries, which flourished in Norman times. The latter declined in the 16th century, and was superseded by hosiery manufacture, which sprang up after the invention of the stocking-loom in 1589.

The earliest evidence of the working of the Nottinghamshire coalfield is from 1259. During the Industrial Revolution the county's reserves of coal and iron ore were much needed, and led to the construction of some of the first experimental wagon-ways in the world. An example of this is the Wollaton wagon-way of 1603-1616, which transported minerals from bell pit mining areas at Strelley and Bilborough. By 1881, 39 collieries were at work in the county. By then mechanised, deeper collieries had opened, though these declined in the late 20th century.

Hops were formerly extensively grown, and Worksop was famous for its liquorice. Numerous cotton mills were erected in Nottinghamshire in the 18th century, and there were silk-mills at Nottingham. The manufacture of tambour lace existed in Nottinghamshire in the 18th century, and was facilitated in the 19th century by the manufacture of machine-made net. ⊠

Oxfordshire

Oxfordshire was recorded as a county in the early years of the 10th century and is situated on land between the River Thames to the south, the Cotswolds to the west, the Chilterns to the east and the Midlands to the north, with areas running south to Henley-on-Thames and north to Banbury.

Historically the area has always had some importance, since it contains valuable agricultural land. The University of Oxford has its origins in 1096, though its collegiate structure did not develop until later on. The university and the city grew in importance during the Middle Ages and early modern period.

The area was part of the Cotswolds wool trade from the 13th century, generating much wealth, particularly in the western portions of the county such as Witney and Chipping Norton.

During the English Civil War, Oxford housed the court of Charles I in 1642, after the king was expelled from London, although there was strong support in the town for the Parliamentarian cause. The town yielded to Parliamentarian forces under General Fairfax in the Siege of Oxford of 1646. It later housed the court of Charles II during the Great Plague of London in 1665–66.

In 1790, the Oxford Canal connected the city with Coventry. For the next 15 years it became one of the most important and profitable transport links in Britain, with most commercial traffic between London

HISTORIC COUNTY BOUNDARIES

1844: Transferred to other counties: part of the parish of Broughton Poggs to Gloucester-shire; the parish of Lillingstone Lovell, the township of Boycott (in the parish of Stowe) and the chapelry of Ackhampstead (in the parish of Lewknor) to Bucking-hamshire

1844: Transferred from other counties: the hamlet of Studeley (in the parish of Beckley), the parish of Caversfield and part of the chapelry of Stratton Audley (in the parish of Bicester) from Buckinghamshire; the tithing and chapelry of Little Faringdon (in the parish of Langford) and part of the parish of Shilton from Berkshire; the parishes of Shenington and Widford from Gloucestershire

1972: the Vale of the White Horse and Didcot joined Oxfordshire from Berkshire

Parishes across two counties: Bucks/Oxon - Ibstone

RECORDS

Oxon records at TheGenealogist.co.uk:

- **Trade directories:** nine directories from 1830 to 1939.
- **Parish registers** for four parishes (see www.thegenealogist.co.uk/coverage/parish-records/oxfordshire/).
- **Land owners:** tithe commutation records and maps.
- **College registers** for the University of Oxford, and specifically Balliol, Brasenose, Exeter, St Peter's Radley, St Mary Magdalen and Wadham Colleges
- **Military records** of the Oxfordshire & Buckinghamshire Light Infantry.
- A collection of **wills**, plus medieval **visitations** from 1566, 1574 and 1634.

SURNAMES

Common Oxfordshire names:

1841	**1911**
HARRIS	HARRIS
GREEN	COX
KING	WEBB
COX	KING
WEBB	ALLEN
COOPER	COOPER
TURNER	TURNER
GARDNER	CLARKE
TOWNSEND	GARDNER
CARTER	BUTLER
HUNT	HUNT
WHEELER	

RESOURCES

- Oxfordshire History Centre, Oxford, www.oxfordshire.gov.uk/cms/public-site/oxfordshire-history-centre
- Oxfordshire Family History Society, www.ofhs.org.uk
- Soldiers of Oxfordshire Museum, Woodstock, www.sofo.org.uk
- Find other resources at www.genuki.org.uk/big/eng/OXF/

and the Midlands using the route. Its principal traffic was coal from Warwickshire. It also carried stone, agricultural products and other goods, until a much more direct route between London and the Midlands, the Grand Junction Canal, was completed in 1805. In 1844, the Great Western Railway linked Oxford with London via Didcot and Reading, and other rail routes soon followed.

The paper mill in Lower Wolvercote, former supplier of paper to the Oxford University Press, was once an important employer. It was in existence by 1720. The publishing industry has been important in Oxford ever since. Morris Motors was founded in Oxford in 1912, and car manufacture continues to this day.

There is a long history of brewing in Oxford. Several of the colleges had private breweries, one of which, at Brasenose, survived until 1889. In the 16th century brewing and malting appear to have been the most popular trades in the city.

The Oxfordshire and Buckinghamshire Light Infantry, the main army unit in the area from 1881 to 1958, was based at Cowley Barracks on Bullingdon Green, Cowley.

Rutland

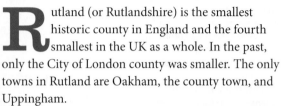

Rutland (or Rutlandshire) is the smallest historic county in England and the fourth smallest in the UK as a whole. In the past, only the City of London county was smaller. The only towns in Rutland are Oakham, the county town, and Uppingham.

The north-western part of the county was recorded as a detached part of Nottinghamshire in the Domesday Book. It was first mentioned as a separate county in 1159, but as late as the 14th century it was referred to as the 'Soke of Rutland'. The office of High Sheriff of Rutland was instituted in 1129, and there has been a Lord Lieutenant of Rutland since at least 1559.

In 1584 Uppingham School, one of the earliest 'public' schools of England, was founded in Rutland with a hospital or almshouse by Archdeacon Robert Johnson. Earl of Rutland and Duke of Rutland are titles in the peerage of England held in the Manners family.

In the 15th century, Rutland was the scene of the Wars of the Roses battle of Loosecoat Field, where in 1470 Edward IV met and defeated the Lincolnshire insurgents near Empingham. There were some disturbances in the county in the reign of Edward VI but there is little evidence of dissatisfaction under the early Stuart kings, although there was obvious disapproval of Charles I's breach with parliament.

When the Civil War broke out, the majority of the leading men of Rutland joined the royalist forces, but its geographical position, especially after the battle of Edgehill, put it definitely in the sphere of the Parliamentary Midland Association.

Rutland covered parts of three poor law unions and rural sanitary districts (RSDs): those of Oakham, Uppingham and Stamford. The registration county of Rutland contained the entirety of Oakham and

HISTORIC COUNTY BOUNDARIES

1972: Rutland was joined administratively with Leicestershire; it was restored as a unitary authority in 1997

RECORDS

Rutland records at TheGenealogist.co.uk:
- **Trade directories:** four directories from 1850 to 1925.
- **Parish registers** for North Luffenham.
- **Land owners:** tithe commutation records and maps.
- **School registers** for Uppingham School, 1824-1913.
- A Northamptonshire and Rutland Calendar of **Wills** 1510-1652.
- Some **Domesday** records, and **visitations** for 1618-19 and 1681-82.

SURNAMES

Common Rutland names:

1841	1911
KING	COOPER
ALLEN	KING
COX	ALLEN
GREEN	CLARKE
HILL	CLARK
RICHARDSON	RICHARDSON
CLARKE	BURTON
WOODS	CHAPMAN
JACKSON	PEACOCK
CHAPMAN	CARTER

RESOURCES

- Leicestershire, Leicester & Rutland Record Office, Wigston (Leics), www.leics.gov.uk/record-office
- Leicestershire & Rutland Family History Society, www.lrfhs.org.uk
- The 58th (Rutlandshire) Regiment of Foot existed from 1755 to 1881 and its records are held in Northamptonshire Regiment and Northamptonshire Yeomanry Collections, Abington Park, Northampton, www.northampton.gov.uk/museums
- Find other resources at www.genuki.org.uk/big/eng/RUT/

Uppingham RSDs, which included several parishes in Leicestershire and Northamptonshire. Rutland gained its own county council by the Local Government Act 1888.

Under the Poor Laws, Oakham Union workhouse was built in 1836–37 at a site to the north-east of the town, with room for 100 paupers. The building later operated as the Catmose Vale Hospital, and now forms part of Oakham School.

In the time of Henry I, Rutland was famed as a hunting county, and for centuries it has been popular as a place of residence for wealthy country gentlemen.

The county grew in prosperity from the 14th century thanks to an increase in sheep farming. Common crops in the county have included wheat, barley and turnips; and Stilton cheese has been made there. There has been no significant history of industry in the county. The manufacture of 'tammy', a fine worsted cloth of good quality, continued until the early 19th century. Trencher tableware was manufactured on a small scale. ✖

Shropshire

S hropshire was established during the division of Saxon Mercia into shires in the 10th century. It is first mentioned in 1006. The border with Wales was only defined in the first half of the 16th century – the hundreds of Oswestry and Pimhill (including Wem), and part of Chirbury had previously formed various lordships in the Welsh Marches.

The origin of the name 'Shropshire' lies in the Old English for Shrewsburyshire. The Normans found it difficult to pronounce so they used 'Salopescira', hence the use of Salop as an abbreviation to this day.

The constant necessity of defending their territories against the Welsh prompted the Norman lords of Shropshire to such enthusiasm for castle-building that out of 186 castles in England no less than 32 are in this county. Various statutory measures to keep the Welsh in check were enforced in the 14th and 15th centuries. Meanwhile Henry 'Hotspur' Percy's rebel army was defeated by the Lancastrians at the Battle of Shrewsbury in 1403.

On the outbreak of the Civil War in the 17th century the Shropshire gentry for the most part declared for the king, who visited Shrewsbury in 1642 and received valuable financial contributions from the inhabitants. Shrewsbury became a refuge for the neighbouring royalist gentry, but was forced to surrender in 1644.

The earliest industries of Shropshire took their rise from its abundant natural resources: the rivers supplying valuable fisheries; the vast forest areas an abundance of timber; and the mineral products of the county had been exploited from remote times. The Domesday Survey mentions salt-works at Ditton Priors, Caynham and Donnington. The lead mines

HISTORIC COUNTY BOUNDARIES

1844: Transferred to other counties: the townships of Halesowen, Cakemore, Hasbury, Hawne, Hill, Illey, Lapal, Ridgacre, Hunnington, Oldbury and Romsley (all in the parish of Halesowen) to Worcestershire

1844: Transferred from other counties: the chapelry of Farlow (in the parish of Stottesdon) in Herefordshire

Parishes across two counties: Salop/Montgomerys – Rhydycroesau, Craignant; Salop/Staffs – Buttonoak, Halfpenny Green, Six Ashes, The Four Alls, Salop/Worcs, Bewdley

RECORDS

Shropshire records at TheGenealogist.co.uk:
- **Trade directories:** seven directories from 1828 to 1940.
- **Parish registers** for more than 100 parishes (see www.thegenealogist.co.uk/coverage/parish-records/shropshire/); and some Catholic registers from Newport.
- **Land owners:** tithe commutation records and some maps.
- **School registers** for Shrewsbury School 1798-1928.
- **Medieval visitations** from 1623.

SURNAMES

Common Shropshire names:

1841	1911
MORRIS	MORRIS
PRICE	PRICE
GRIFFITHS	GRIFFITHS
LLOYD	LEWIS
ROGERS	HUGHES
DAVIS	LLOYD
POWELL	OWEN
OWEN	ROGERS
RICHARDS	POWELL
	MORGAN

RESOURCES

- Shropshire Archives, Shrewsbury, www.shropshire.gov.uk/archives/
- Shropshire Family History Society, www.sfhs.org.uk
- Shropshire Regimental Museum, Shrewsbury, www.shropshireregimentalmuseum.co.uk
- Find other resources at www.genuki.org.uk/big/eng/SAL/

of Shelve and Stiperstones were worked by the Romans, and there was also a lead mine at Shelve in the 13th century. In 1260 a licence was granted to dig coal in the Clee Hills. Iron was also dug there and at Wombridge in the 16th century. Wenlock had a famous copper-mine in the reign of Richard II, and in the l6th century was noted for its limestone.

As the forest areas were gradually cleared and brought under cultivation, the county became more exclusively agricultural. In 1343 Shropshire wool was rated at a higher value than that of almost any other English county. A prosperous clothing trade arose about Shrewsbury and Bridgnorth, and Oswestry was famous in the l6th century for its 'Welsh cottons'.

Coalbrookdale, a small area of Shropshire, has been claimed as the birthplace of the Industrial Revolution, because of Abraham Darby's development of coke-smelting and iron-founding there in the early 18th century. Ironbridge is where the world's first iron bridge was constructed, to link Broseley with Madeley and the Black Country, and Ditherington is where the world's first iron-framed building was built, the Ditherington Flaxmill. Later, Broseley and Madeley became notable for their continuation of trade in the field of bricks and tiles, which became a staple to the booming building trade, and millions of Broseley clay pipes were exported across the British Empire. ▩

Somerset

The first known use of the name Somerset (a name derived from Somerton, briefly the county town in medieval times) dates from the 7th century, making the county (along with Hampshire, Wiltshire and Dorset) one of the oldest still existing units of local government in the world.

The caves of the Mendip Hills were settled during the Palaeolithic period, and contain extensive archaeological sites such as those at Cheddar Gorge. Bones from Gough's Cave have been dated to 12000 BC, and modern descendents have been identified by DNA, still living in the area.

By the early eighth century King Ine of Wessex had pushed the boundaries of the West Saxon kingdom far enough west to include Somerset. After the Norman Conquest, fortifications such as Dunster Castle were used for control and defence. Somerset contains HM Prison Shepton Mallet, England's oldest prison still in use, dating to 1610.

In the English Civil War, Somerset was largely Parliamentarian (although Dunster was a Royalist stronghold), with key engagements being the sieges of Taunton and the Battle of Langport. In 1685, the Duke of Monmouth led the Monmouth Rebellion in which Somerset people fought against James II. The rebels landed at Lyme Regis and travelled north hoping to capture Bristol and Bath, Puritan soldiers damaged the west front of Wells Cathedral, and for a time stabled their horses in the nave, but they were defeated in the Battle of Sedgemoor at Westonzoyland, often held to be the last pitched battle fought in England. The Bloody Assizes which followed saw the losers being sentenced to death or transportation.

Among a close-knit group of Quaker families established in Street in the mid-17th century were the Clarks: Cyrus started a business in sheepskin rugs, later joined by his brother James, who introduced the

HISTORIC COUNTY BOUNDARIES

1844: Transferred to other counties: the parish of Holwell to Dorset
Parishes across two counties: Devon/Somerset - Bishopswood, Malmsmead, Oldways End;
Dorset/Somerset - Chard Junction

RECORDS

Somerset records at TheGenealogist.co.uk:
- **Trade directories:** Kelly's 1897 Somersetshire Directory.
- **Parish registers** for more than 100 parishes (see www.thegenealogist.co.uk/coverage/parish-records/somerset/).
- **Land owners:** tithe commutation records.
- **School registers** for Kingswood School.
- 1832 **electoral registers** and an 1855 Bath poll book
- 1531 & 1573 medieval **visitations**.

SURNAMES

Common Somerset names:

1841	1911
BAKER	BAKER
HILL	DAVIS
DAVIS	HILL
COX	COX
PARSONS	HARRIS
TUCKER	PARSONS
HARRIS	JAMES
PALMER	COLES
COOK	TUCKER
COLES	PALMER
JAMES	STONE

RESOURCES

- Somerset Heritage Centre, Taunton, www1.somerset.gov.uk/archives/
- Somerset & Dorset Family History Society, www.sdfhs.org
- Weston-Super-Mare & District FHS, www.wsmfhs.org.uk
- Bristol & Avon FHS, www.bafhs.org.uk
- Somerset Military Museum (at the Museum of Somerset), Taunton, www.museumofsomerset.org.uk
- Find other resources at www.genuki.org.uk/big/eng/SOM/

production of woollen slippers and, later, boots and shoes. C&J Clark still has its headquarters in Street, but shoes are no longer manufactured there.

The Industrial Revolution spelled the end for many of Somerset's cottage industries. Farming continued to flourish, however, and the Bath and West of England Society was founded in 1777 to improve farming methods. Coal mining was an important industry in north Somerset during the 18th and 19th centuries, and by 1800 it was prominent in Radstock. The Somerset coalfield reached its peak production by the 1920s, but all the pits had closed by 1973. Further west, the Brendon Hills were mined for iron ore in the late 19th century; this was taken by rail to Watchet Harbour for shipment to the furnaces at Ebbw Vale.

During World War Two the county was a base for troops preparing for the D-Day landings. Some of the hospitals which were built for the casualties of the war remain in use. The Taunton Stop Line was set up to repel a potential German invasion. The remains of its pill boxes can still be seen along the coast, and south through Ilminster and Chard. A number of decoy towns were constructed in Somerset in World War Two to protect Bristol and other towns at night.

Staffordshire

The county of Staffordshire has been a distinct entity since the early 10th century, when Stafford became the capital of Mercia.

Historically, Staffordshire was divided into the five hundreds, Totmonslow, Pirehill, Offlow, Cuttleston and Seisdo. In 1553 Lichfield became a separate county, remaining so until 1888.

Northern Staffordshire is to a large extent moorland (the county is home to the highest village in Britain, Flash), less attractive to early settlers, while southern Staffordshire was largely forested, covered particularly by Kinver and Cannock Forests. Throughout the entire county there are important coalfields. In the southern part there are also rich iron ore deposits. The soil is chiefly clay and agriculture was not highly developed in the region until the mechanisation of farming.

Staffordshire is most famous for its potteries. The traditional 'six towns' of the Staffordshire Potteries – now forming the city of Stoke-on-Trent – were Tunstall, Burslem, Hanley, Stoke, Fenton and Longton. North Staffordshire started to become a centre of ceramic production in the early 17th century, due to the local availability of clay, salt, lead and coal.

HISTORIC COUNTY BOUNDARIES

1844: Transferred to other counties: the parishes of Broome and Clent transferred to Worcestershire

1844: Transferred from other counties: part of the township of Foston and Scropton (in the parish of Scropton) in Derbyshire

1889: The extra-parochial place of Dudley Castle, formerly in Worcestershire, became a detached part of Staffordshire, surrounded by the county borough of Dudley, itself a detached part of Worcestershire. In 1929, it was absorbed by the civil parish and county borough of Dudley, Worcestershire

1972: The county lost the conurbations of Wolverhampton, Walsall and West Bromwich to the West Midlands.

Parishes across two counties: Cheshire/Staffs – Balterley Heath, Congleton Edge, Mount Pleasant, Mow Cop; Derbys/Staffs – Edingale; Salop/Staffs – Buttonoak, Halfpenny Green, Six Ashes, The Four Alls, Salop/Worcs, Bewdley; Staffs/Warks – Bearwood, Gib Heath, Lozells, New Oscott, Tamworth, Witton; Staffs/Worcs – Blackheath, Burnt Tree, Oakham, Overend, Whiteheath Gate

RECORDS

Staffs records at TheGenealogist.co.uk:

- **Trade directories:** six directories from 1835 to 1901.
- **Parish registers** for more than 10 parishes (see www.thegenealogist.co.uk/coverage/parish-records/staffordshire/).
- **Land owners:** tithe commutation records and maps.
- Lichfield **wills** from 1516 to 1652.

SURNAMES

Common Staffordshire names:

1841	1911
COOPER	COOPER
TURNER	TURNER
DAVIS	HILL
HILL	WALKER
WALKER	BAILEY
GREEN	HUGHES
HOUSE	PRICE
BAKER	
JACKSON	

RESOURCES

- Staffordshire & Stoke-on-Trent Archive Service has record offices in Stafford, Stoke-on-Trent, Lichfield and Burton, www.staffordshire.gov.uk/leisure/archives
- Birmingham & Midland Society for Genealogy & Heraldry has branches in Newcastle-under-Lyme, Burton-on-Trent and Wolverhampton, www.bmsgh.org
- Burntwood Family History Group, www.bfhg.org.uk
- Staffordshire Regiment Museum, Whittington, www.staffordshireregimentmuseum.com
- Find other resources at www.genuki.org.uk/big/eng/STS/

Hundreds of companies produced decorative or industrial ceramic items.

The boom came after the discovery in 1720, by potter John Astbury of Shelton, that adding heated and ground flint powder to the local reddish clay could create a more attractive white or cream ware. The flint was sourced from either the south coast of England or France, and then shipped to the port of Liverpool or Shardlow on the River Trent. It was then ground by local watermills or commercial flint grinding mills in either the Churnet Valley or Moddershall Valley. Until the process was improved, many pottery workers suffered from silicosis. (See www.thepotteries.org for more information, including genealogy resources.)

With the coming of the railway distribution of pottery products from the 1840s, mainly by the London and North Western Railway and Midland Railway, there was a considerable increase in business. The Chartist 1842 General Strike was ignited by striking collieries in the Potteries and led to the 1842 Pottery Riots.

Primitive Methodism was also founded in Staffordshire by Hugh Bourne at a public gathering in the village of Mow Cop. In 1801 he reformed the Wesleyan Methodist service by conducting it outside, and co-founded a chapel in Tunstall. 🕱

Suffolk

The county of Suffolk (meaning 'southern folk') was formed from the south part of the kingdom of East Anglia which had been settled by the Angles in the latter half of the 5th century. In the east of the county is Sutton Hoo, the site of one of England's most significant Anglo-Saxon archaeological finds: a ship burial containing a collection of treasures including a sword of state, gold and silver bowls and jewellery.

Suffolk suffered severely from Danish incursions, and after the Treaty of Wedmore became a part of the Danelaw. Although it was reckoned as distinct from Norfolk in the Domesday survey of 1086, the fiscal administration of Norfolk and Suffolk remained under a single sheriff until 1575. The boundary of the county has undergone very little change, though its area has been considerably affected by coast erosion.

In 1173 the Earl of Leicester landed at Walton with an army of Flemings and was joined by Hugh Bigod against Henry II. In 1317 and the succeeding years a great part of the county was in arms for Thomas of Lancaster. In 1381 there was a serious rising of the peasantry chiefly in the neighbourhood of Bury St Edmunds. Although the county was for the most part Yorkist it took little part in the Wars of the Roses. It was from Suffolk that Mary drew the army which supported her claim to the throne. In the Civil Wars the county was for the most part Parliamentarian, and joined the Association of the Eastern Counties for defence against the Catholic Royalists.

Suffolk was originally among the most populous of English counties, perhaps owing to its proximity to the continent. Fishing fleets left its ports to bring back cod and ling from Iceland and herring and mackerel from the North Sea. From the 14th to the 17th century it was among the chief manufacturing counties of England owing to its cloth-weaving industry, which was at the height of its prosperity during the 15th century.

HISTORIC COUNTY BOUNDARIES

Parishes across two counties: Cambs/Suffolk – Kennett, Kennett End, Landwade, Newmarket; Essex/Suffolk – Haverhill; Norfolk/Suffolk – Brandon, Rushford, Thetford

RECORDS

Suffolk records at TheGenealogist.co.uk:
- **Trade directories:** eight directories from 1844 to 1937.
- **Parish registers** for more than 40 parishes (see www.thegenealogist.co.uk/coverage/parish-records/suffolk/).
- **Land owners:** tithe commutation records and some maps.
- **School registers** for Bury St Edmunds Grammar School List
- **Poll books** for 1710, 1790, 1832, 1830
- A calendar of **wills** 1383-1604
- **Visitations** of Suffolk 1561, 1577, 1612

SURNAMES

Common Suffolk names:

1841	1911
CLARKE	CLARKE
COOK	COOK
KING	KING
COOPER	TURNER
BAKER	COOPER
GREEN	BAKER
NUNN	WARD
TURNER	NUNN
READ	MOORE
WOODS	HAMMOND
WARD	LAST

RESOURCES

- Suffolk Record Office, Bury St Edmunds, www.suffolk.gov.uk/culture-heritage-and-leisure/suffolk-record-office/
- Suffolk Family History Society, www.suffolkfhs.org.uk
- Alde Valley Suffolk Family History Group, aldevalleyfamilyhistorygroup.onesuffolk.net
- Felixstowe FHS, www.itgen.co.uk/ffhs/
- The Suffolk Regiment Museum, Bury St Edmunds, www.suffolkregiment.org/museum.html
- Find other resources at www.genuki.org.uk/big/eng/SFK/

In the 17th and 18th centuries its agricultural resources provide the rapidly growing metropolis of London with food. In the 18th century Suffolk was famed for its dairy products, but the high prices of grain during the wars of the French Revolution led to the extensive breaking up of its pastures, and it has since been one of the principal grain-growing counties in England.

In the 19th century, various textile industries, such as the manufacture of sail-cloth, coconut fibre, horse-hair and clothing were established; silk-weavers migrated to Suffolk from Spitalfields, and early in the 19th century an important china factory flourished at Lowestoft.

In the arts, Suffolk is noted for having been the home to two of England's best regarded painters, Thomas Gainsborough and John Constable – the Stour Valley area is known as 'Constable Country' – and one of its most noted composers, Benjamin Britten. Significant ecclesiastical figures from Suffolk include Simon Sudbury, a former Archbishop of Canterbury; the Tudor-era Catholic prelate Cardinal Thomas Wolsey; and author, poet and Benedictine monk John Lydgate. ✠

Surrey

During the 5th and 6th centuries Surrey was conquered and settled by Saxons. In the 7th century, it became a frontier area disputed between the kingdoms of Kent, Essex, Sussex, Wessex and Mercia, until its permanent absorption by Wessex in 825.

After the Battle of Hastings, the Norman army advanced through Kent into Surrey, where they defeated an English force which attacked them at Southwark, before proceeding westwards on a circuitous march to reach London from the north-west. During King John's struggle with the barons, Magna Carta was issued in June 1215 at Runnymede in Surrey.

Surrey had little political or economic importance in the Middle Ages. It was not the main power-base of any major aristocratic family or the seat of a bishopric. Its agricultural wealth was limited by its soil varieties. Its forested North Downs and the Wealden plain were of timber, charcoal and hunting use. Significant prosperity focused in the later Middle Ages on the production of woollen cloth, England's main export industry, which in Surrey saw much of its manufacture in Guildford.

Surrey's cloth industry declined in the 16th century, and effectively collapsed in the 17th. The introduction of new furnace technology in the early 17th century led to a brief expansion of the iron industry in the Weald, until the mines were worked out. This period also saw the emergence of important new industries, centred on the valley of the Till-ingbourne. The production of brass goods and wire in this area was relatively short-lived, but the manufacture of paper and gunpowder proved more enduring. For a time in the mid-17th century the Surrey

HISTORIC COUNTY BOUNDARIES

1889: Lambeth, Southwark, Wandsworth, and parts of Lewisham and Bromley became London boroughs

1965: Croydon, Kingston upon Thames, Merton, Sutton and Richmond upon Thames south of the River Thames became London boroughs

Parishes across two counties: Kent/Surrey - Anerley, Honor Oak, Nunhead, Penge, Spring Park; Surrey/Sussex - Black Corner, Copthorne, Effingham Park, Tinsley Green

RECORDS

Surrey records at TheGenealogist.co.uk:
- **Trade directories:** 1839 Surrey Pigot's Directory and 1938 Surrey Kelly's Directory.
- **Parish registers** for around 25 parishes (see www.thegenealogist.co.uk/coverage/parish-records/surrey/).
- **Land owners:** tithe commutation records and maps.
- **School registers** for Epsom College Register and Whitgift Grammar School.
- An index of **wills**, 1484-1490.
- Medieval **visitations** from 1530 and 1662-68.

SURNAMES

Common Surrey names:

1841	1911
BAKER	BAKER
KING	KING
TURNER	COOPER
COOPER	MARTIN
KNIGHT	TURNER
LEE	HARRIS
STEVENS	KNIGHT
YOUNG	CLARK
MARTIN	HILL
WOODS	
HILL	

RESOURCES

- Surrey History Centre, Woking, www.surreycc.gov.uk/surreyhistorycentre
- East Surrey Family History Society, www.eastsurreyfhs.org.uk
- West Surrey Family History Society, www.wsfhs.co.uk
- Surrey Infantry Museum, Clandon Park, www.queensroyalsurreys.org.uk/new_museum/new_museum.shtml
- Find other resources at www.genuki.org.uk/big/eng/SRY/

mills were the main producers of gunpowder in England. The Wey Navigation, opened in 1653, was one of England's first canal systems.

Surrey almost entirely escaped the direct impact of fighting during the main phase of the English Civil War in 1642-6, but had a prominent role in the development of the radical political movements unleashed by the civil war. In October 1647 the first manifesto of what became known as the Leveller movement was drafted at Guildford.

Until the late 18th century Surrey, apart from its north-eastern corner, was sparsely populated and somewhat rustic, despite its proximity to the capital. Communications began to improve, and the influence of London to increase, with the development of turnpike roads and a stagecoach system. A far more profound transformation followed with the arrival of the railways, beginning in the late 1830s. Commuting brought explosive growth to Surrey's population and wealth, and tied its economy and society inextricably to London.

In 1849 Brookwood Cemetery was established near Woking to serve the population of London, connected to the capital by its own railway service. It soon developed into the largest burial ground in the world. Woking was also the site of Britain's first crematorium, opened in 1878. 🏴

Sussex (East & West)

Sussex has three main geographic sub-regions, each oriented approximately east to west. In the south-west of the county lies the fertile and densely populated coastal plain. North of this lie the rolling chalk hills of the South Downs, beyond which lies the well-wooded Sussex Weald. The name derives from the Anglo-Saxon Kingdom of the South Saxons. The region is rich in prehistoric and Roman remains.

After the Battle of Hastings, Sussex experienced some of the greatest changes of any English county under the Normans. The county's existing sub-divisions, known as rapes, were made into 'castleries' and each territory was given to one of William's most trusted barons.

During the Hundred Years War, Sussex found itself on the front line, convenient both for intended invasions and retaliatory expeditions by licensed French pirates. Hastings, Rye and Winchelsea were all burnt during this period and all three became part of the Cinque Ports, a loose federation for supplying ships for the country's security.

At the beginning of the 19th century the deteriorating conditions of work for agricultural labourers eventually triggered 'Swing riots' in Sussex and Kent.

Much of the Sussex Weald consists of clay and is often broken up into to small irregular fields and woods by the topography, making it unsuitable for intensive arable farming. The chalk downlands were traditionally grazed by large numbers of small Southdown sheep, suited to the low fertility of the pasture, until the coming of artificial fertiliser made cereal growing worthwhile.

There have been fishing fleets, notably at Rye and Hastings, for centuries. The Weald also had an iron-working industry since the Roman period, aided

HISTORIC COUNTY BOUNDARIES

1844: Transferred from other counties: the tithings of North Ambersham and South Ambersham (both in the parish of Steep), and part of the parish of Rogate, from Hampshire

1972: The historic county was separated into the administrative counties of West and East Sussex

Parishes across two counties: Hants/Sussex – Hill Brow, Nursted, Rake; Kent/Sussex – Lamberhurst; Surrey/Sussex – Black Corner, Copthorne, Effingham Park, Tinsley Green

RECORDS

Sussex records at TheGenealogist.co.uk:

- **Trade directories:** six directories from 1839 to 1938.
- **Parish registers** for 6 parishes, including Brighton & Hove (see www.thegenealogist. co.uk/coverage/parish-records/sussex/); plus a searchable printed book of Catholic Mission Registers for Cowdray, Easebourne and Midhurst.
- **Land owners:** tithe commutation records.
- **School registers** for Windlesham House near Washington.
- An 1820 **poll book**
- The Chichester Calendar of **Wills** 1482-1800.

SURNAMES

Common Sussex names:

1841	1911
BAKER	BAKER
MARTIN	MARTIN
MITCHELL	KNIGHT
KNIGHT	KING
TURNER	MITCHELL
KING	TURNER
COLLINS	RICHARDSON
RICHARDSON	STEVENS
MILLS	GREEN
STEVENS	PARSONS
COOPER	COLLINS
CARTER	COOPER
PARKER	

RESOURCES

- East Sussex Record Office is at The Keep, Brighton, www.thekeep.info; West Sussex Record Office is in Chichester, www.westsussex.gov.uk/leisure-recreation-and-community/history-and-heritage/west-sussex-record-office/
- Sussex Family History Group, www.sfhg.org.uk
- Eastbourne & District (Family Roots) Family History Society, www.eastbournefhs.org.uk
- Hastings & Rother FHS, www.hrfhs.org.uk
- Royal Sussex Regimental Museum, Eastbourne, www.eastbournemuseums.co.uk/royal-sussex-regiment.aspxc
- Find other resources at www.genuki.org.uk/big/eng/SSX/

by its large supply of wood, all smelting being done with charcoal until the middle of the 18th century.

The glass-making industry started on the Sussex/Surrey border in the early 13th century and flourished until the 17th century. The mid Sussex area had a thriving clay industry in the first quarter of the 20th century.

The Sussex coast was greatly modified by the social movement of sea bathing for health, which became fashionable among the wealthy in the second half of the 18th century. Resorts developed all along the coast, including at Brighton, Hastings, Worthing and Bognor.

During World War One, on the eve of the Battle of the Somme on 30 June 1916, the Royal Sussex Regiment took part in the Battle of the Boar's Head – the day subsequently became known as The Day Sussex Died, with more than 350 men killed in less than five hours. In World War Two, Sussex found itself part of the country's front line with its airfields playing a key role in the Battle of Britain and with its towns being some of the most frequently bombed. 🞜

Warwickshire

Warwickshire is a landlocked county in the centre of England, famous for being the birthplace of William Shakespeare and George Eliot. The market towns of northern and eastern Warwickshire were industrialised in the 19th century; the south of the county remains largely rural and sparsely populated, and includes a small area of the Cotswolds.

Much of western Warwickshire, including that area now forming part of Coventry, Solihull and Birmingham, was covered by the ancient Forest of Arden (most of which was cut down to provide fuel for industrialisation).

Warwickshire came into being as a division of the kingdom of Mercia in the early 11th century. The Norman period saw the foundation of many castles, including Warwick and Kenilworth.

During the Middle Ages Warwickshire was dominated by Coventry, which was at the time one of the most important cities in England due to its textiles trade and location in the heart of the country.

Some of the Gunpowder Plot conspirators came from Warwickshire and much of the plotting took place in the county. Warwickshire also played a key part in the English Civil War (generally on the Parliamentarian side), with the Battle of Edgehill and other skirmishes taking place there.

During the 18th and 19th centuries Warwickshire became one of Britain's

---

BOUNDARY CHANGES

1844: Transferred to other counties: the township of Tutnall and Cobley (in the parish of Tardebigge) to Worcestershire

1844: Transferred from other counties: the parishes of Little Compton and Sutton-under-Brailes from Gloucestershire

1889: The cities Birmingham and Coventry and the town of Solihull went to the West Midlands

1931: Ilmington, Stretton-on-Fosse and Whitchurch formed a detached part of Warwickshire, separated from the main part of the county by an exclave of four Worcestershire parishes. In 1931, the intervening area of Worcestershire was transferred to Warwickshire, so that the three parishes became joined to the rest of the county

Parishes across two counties: Staffs/Warks – Bearwood, Gib Heath, Lozells, New Oscott, Tamworth, Witton; Leics/Warks – No Man's Heath; Warks/Worcs – Astwood Bank, Cookhill, Garrets Green, Headless Cross, New End, Portway, The Ridgeway, Trueman's Heath

RECORDS

Warks records at TheGenealogist.co.uk:
- **Trade directories:** ten directories from 1835 to 1933.
- **Parish registers** for more than 20 parishes (see www.thegenealogist.co.uk/coverage/parish-records/warwickshire/); transcriptions from Knowle; Catholic registers for Wootton Wawen.
- **Land owners:** tithe commutation records and maps.
- **School registers** for Rugby School from the 17th to 20th centuries, and medieval **visitations** of the county from 1619.

SURNAMES

Common Warwickshire names:

1841	1911
GREEN	HARRIS
WARD	CLARKE
HARRIS	HILL
HILL	WARD
BAKER	COOPER
COOPER	MOORE
PARKER	MORRIS
WALKER	TURNER
ALLEN	

RESOURCES

- Warwickshire Record Office, Warwick, http://heritage.warwickshire.gov.uk/warwickshire-county-record-office/
- University of Warwick Modern Records Office, Coventry, modernrecords.warwick.ac.uk
- Birmingham & Midland Society for Genealogy & Heraldry, www.bmsgh.org
- Coventry FHS, www.covfhs.org.uk
- Nuneaton & North Warwickshire FHS, www.nnwfhs.org.uk
- Rugby FH Group, www.rugbyfhg.co.uk
- Find other Warwickshire resources at www.genuki.org.uk/big/eng/WAR/

foremost industrial counties. The coalfields of northern Warwickshire were among the most productive in the country, and greatly enhanced the industrial growth of Coventry and Birmingham. Other major industries in the county included textiles, engineering and cement production.

One notable exception was the town of Leamington Spa, which grew from a small village to a medium-sized town during the 19th century on the back of the fashionable spa water tourist movement of the time.

Census data reflects industrial expansion, with the population surging from 400,000 in 1841 to over a million in 1911. The earlier census shows the importance of textiles, with many people working as weavers, dressmakers and tailors; 1911 reflects the rise of coal mining.

Warwickshire became a centre of the national canal system, with major arterial routes such as the Oxford Canal, the Coventry Canal and what is now the Grand Union Canal being constructed through the county.

One of the first inter-city railway lines, the London and Birmingham Railway, ran through Warwickshire. During the 19th century, the county developed a dense railway network. ▓

Wiltshire

T he county of Wiltshire was formed in Saxon times, although the huge number of prehistoric remains (most notably Avebury, Silbury Hill and Stonehenge) are testament to its far older settlement. The Normans' Domesday Survey mentioned 40 hundreds, almost half of which remain barely altered today.

The inhabitants of Wiltshire have always been addicted to industrious rather than warlike pursuits, and the political history of the county is notably peaceable in comparison to many other regions. After the completion of the Domesday Survey, Salisbury was the scene of a great council, in which all the landholders took oaths of allegiance to the king.

In the Civil War of the 17th century, Wiltshire actively supported the parliamentary cause; Marlborough was captured for the king in 1642 and the Battle of Roundway Down, a decisive Royalist victory, was fought near Devizes. Before the Glorious Revolution which brought William of Orange to the throne, King James II gathered his main forces, altogether about 19,000 men, at Salisbury, James himself arriving there on 19 November 1688.

At the time of Domesday the industrial pursuits of Wiltshire were almost exclusively agricultural; 390 mills are mentioned, and vineyards at Tollard Royal and Lacock. In the succeeding centuries sheep farming was vigorously pursued, and two Cistercian monasteries exported wool to the Florentine and Flemish markets in the 13th and 14th centuries. Wiltshire at this time was already reckoned among the chief of the clothing counties, the principal centres of the industry being Bradford

HISTORIC COUNTY BOUNDARIES

1844: Transferred to other counties: part of the parochial chapelry of Hurst (in the parish of Sonning), and parts of the parishes of Shinfield and Wokingham, to Berkshire; the parishes of Kingswood and Poulton to Gloucestershire

1844: Transferred from other counties: part of the parish of Inglesham in Berkshire; the parish of Minety in Gloucestershire

Parishes across two counties: Berks/Wilts – Shalbourne; Dorset/Wilts – Queen Oak; Hants/Wilts – Bramshaw, Brook, Canada, Faberstown, Furzley, Henley, North Charford, North Tidworth, Tangley Bottom, West Dean

RECORDS

Wiltshire records at TheGenealogist.co.uk:

- **Trade directories:** four directories from 1899 to 1923.
- **Parish registers** for almost 80 parishes (see www.thegenealogist.co.uk/coverage/parish-records/wiltshire/).
- **Land owners:** tithe commutation records and some maps.
- **School registers** for Marlborough College.
- **Visitation records** from 1623

SURNAMES

Common Wiltshire names:

1841	1911
KING	PEARCE
DAVIS	DAVIS
PEARCE	KING
NEWMAN	WEBB
WEBB	HUNT
HARRIS	BAKER
BAILEY	COOK
COOK	CARTER
WATTS	HARRIS
BAKER	BAILEY
YOUNG	WHEELER

RESOURCES

- Wiltshire and Swindon History Centre, Chippenham, www.wshc.eu
- Wiltshire Family History Society, www.wiltshirefhs.co.uk
- Royal Gloucestershire, Berkshire and Wiltshire Regiment Museum, Salisbury, www.thewardrobe.org.uk
- Find other resources at www.genuki.org.uk/big/eng/WIL/

on Avon, Malmesbury, Trowbridge, Devizes and Chippenham.

In the 16th century Devizes was noted for its blankets, Warminster had a famous corn market, and cheese was extensively made in north Wiltshire. Amesbury was famous for its tobacco pipe manufacture in the 16th century. The clothing trade went through a period of great depression in the 17th century, partly owing to the constant outbreaks of plague. Linen, cotton, gloves and cutlery were also manufactured in the county, silk at Malmesbury and carpets at Wilton.

In 1794 it was decided at a meeting in Devizes to raise a body of ten independent troops for the county, which formed the basis for what would become the Royal Wiltshire Yeomanry, which served with distinction during the Boer War and both world wars.

Around 1800 the Kennet and Avon Canal was built through Wiltshire providing a route for transporting cargoes from Bristol to London until the development of the Great Western Railway. The Swindon Works of the Great Western Railway was one of the largest covered areas in the world, and its remains are among the most significant of Victorian engineering works in the world. Swindon has also been significant in other manufacturing, such as the car industry. ✠

Worcestershire

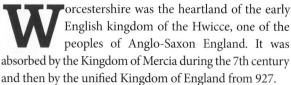

orcestershire was the heartland of the early English kingdom of the Hwicce, one of the peoples of Anglo-Saxon England. It was absorbed by the Kingdom of Mercia during the 7th century and then by the unified Kingdom of England from 927.

Worcestershire was the site of the Battle of Evesham in which Simon de Montfort was killed on 4 August 1265.

In 1642, the first major skirmish of the Civil War, the Battle of Powick Bridge – close to Worcester – occurred when a cavalry troop of about 1,000 Royalists commanded by Prince Rupert, a German nephew of the King and one of the leading cavalry commanders of the war, defeated a Parliamentary cavalry detachment under the command of Colonel John Brown. Worcestershire was again the focus of the Civil War when it was effectively ended by Cromwell's victory at the Battle of Worcester on 3 September 1651.

During the Middle Ages, much of the county's economy was based on

HISTORIC COUNTY BOUNDARIES

1844: Transferred to other counties: the parish of Icomb (including the hamlet of Church Icomb), and the hamlets of Alstone and Little Washbourne (both in the parish of Overbury), to Gloucestershire

1844: Transferred from other counties: the parishes of Broom and Clent from Staffordshire; the townships of Halesowen, Cakemore, Hasbury, Hawne, Hill, Illey, Lapal, Ridgacre, Hunnington, Oldbury and Romsley (all in the parish of Halesowen) from Shropshire; the chapelry of Rochford (in the parish of Tenbury) from Gloucestershire

1889: Dudley became a county borough, but remained a detached part of Worcestershire for non-administrative reasons. In 1966, the county borough absorbed surrounding areas of the administrative county of Staffordshire, and from that date was included in the latter

1893: The parish of Edvin Loach was transferred to Herefordshire

1931: Cutsdean, Blockley, Daylesford and Evenlode transferred to Gloucestershire

1972: The county was merged with Herefordshire to form a large single administrative county of Hereford and Worcester, which in 1998 was reverted to the original historical counties. Some changes in borders occurred with some areas such as Halesowen, Stourbridge, and the exclave of Dudley, becoming part of the West Midlands.

Parishes across two counties: Gloucs/Worcs – Honeybourne; Herefords/Worcs – West Malvern, Wynds Point; Staffs/Worcs – Blackheath, Burnt Tree, Oakham, Overend, Whiteheath Gate; Warks/Worcs – Astwood Bank, Cookhill, Garrets Green, Headless Cross, New End, Portway, The Ridgeway, Trueman's Heath

RECORDS

Worcs records at TheGenealogist.co.uk:

- **Trade directories:** seven directories from 1835 to 1901.
- **Parish registers** for more than 100 parishes (see www.thegenealogist.co.uk/coverage/parish-records/worcestershire/).
- **Land owners:** tithe commutation records and maps.
- **School registers** for Malvern College.
- An 1832-3 register of **electors**.
- Indexes of **wills** from 1451 to 1652.
- Medieval **visitations** from 1682-1683.

SURNAMES

Common Worcestershire names:

1841	1911
DAVIS	HILL
HILL	HARRIS
PRICE	DAVIS
HARRIS	PRICE
GREEN	MORRIS
MORRIS	COOPER
WALKER	CLARKE
COOK	HUGHES
TURNER	
GRIFFITHS	

RESOURCES

- Worcestershire Archive & Archaeology Service (The Hive), Worcester, www.thehiveworcester.org
- Birmingham & Midland Society for Genealogy & Heraldry, www.bmsgh.org
- Malvern Family History Society, www.mfhs.org.uk
- Worcestershire Regimental Collection, Worcester, www.wfrmuseum.org.uk/worcs_museum.htm
- Find other resources at www.genuki.org.uk/big/eng/WOR/

the wool trade, and many areas of its dense forests, such as Malvern Chase, were royal hunting grounds.

In the 19th century, Worcester was a centre for the manufacture of gloves; the town of Kidderminster became a centre for carpet manufacture, and Redditch specialised in the manufacture of needles, springs and hooks. Droitwich, situated on large deposits of salt, was a centre of salt production from Roman times.

These old industries have since declined, to be replaced by other, more varied light industry. The county is also home to the world's oldest continually published newspaper, *Berrow's Journal*, established in 1690. Malvern was one of the centres of the 19th century rise in English spa towns due to Malvern water being believed to be very pure.

Fruit farming and the cultivation of hops were traditional agricultural activities in much of the county. During the latter half of the 20th century, this largely declined with the exception southern area of the county around the Vale of Evesham, where orchards are still worked on a commercial scale.

The original Worcestershire sauce, a savoury condiment made by Lea and Perrins, is made in Worcester, and the now closed Royal Porcelain works was based in the city.

Yorkshire

Early inhabitants of Yorkshire were Celts, who formed two separate tribes, the Brigantes and the Parisi. The Brigantes controlled territory which later became all of the North Riding of Yorkshire and the West Riding of Yorkshire; the Parisi controlled the area that would become the East Riding. In the last centuries of the Roman empire, the fortified city of Eboracum (now York) was named as capital of Britannia Inferior and joint-capital of all Roman Britain.

After the Romans left, small Celtic kingdoms arose in Yorkshire; in the early 7th century, King Edwin of Northumbria annexed the region. An army of Danish Vikings invaded Northumbrian territory in 866 AD. The Danes conquered what is now York and renamed it Jórvík, making it the capital city of a new Danish kingdom under the same name, the only truly Viking territory established on mainland Britain. It lasted for around a century, until the Wessex kings again placed Yorkshire in Northumbria. The division of Yorkshire into three historic 'Ridings' (North, East and West) was made by the Danes (South Yorkshire is a modern division, split off from the West Riding in 1972).

The people of the region rebelled against the Normans in September 1069, enlisting Sweyn II of Denmark. They tried to take back York, but the Normans burnt it. What followed was the Harrying of the North ordered by William. From York to Durham, crops, domestic animals, and farming tools were scorched. Many villages between the towns were burnt and local people were indiscriminately murdered. Families starved to death and thousands of peasants died of cold and hunger.

The population of Yorkshire later boomed until hit by famine in the years between 1315 and 1322. The Black Death reached Yorkshire by 1349, killing around a third of the population.

HISTORIC COUNTY BOUNDARIES

1972: the three ridings of Yorkshire were replaced by North, South and West Yorkshire, along with Humberside

Parishes across two counties: Lancs/Yorkshire - Mossley; Lincs/Yorks - Eastoft, Garthorpe, Fockerby; Notts/Yorks - Bawtry

RECORDS

Yorkshire records at TheGenealogist.co.uk:
- **Trade directories:** around 30 directories from 1830 to 1936.
- **Parish registers** for more than 80 parishes (see www.thegenealogist.co.uk/coverage/parish-records/yorkshire/).
- **Land owners:** tithe commutation records and maps.
- **School registers** for Bootham School, Giggleswick School, Leeds Grammar School and Sedbergh School.
- Some **Domesday** records.
- **Freemen** of York from 1272-1759.
- **Militia and military** records of the West Riding Yorkshire Territorials, the 15th Foot Regiment (Yorkshire East Riding), the 19th Foot Regiment (Yorkshire North Riding) and The Green Howards.
- Various **poll books** from the 18th and 19th century.
- Medieval **visitations** from the late 16th and 17th centuries.
- Indexes of **wills** from the 14th to 17th centuries.

SURNAMES

Common Yorkshire names:

1841
WALKER
JACKSON
THOMPSON
SHAW
WILKINSON
HARRISON
GREEN
WATSON
BARKER
ATKINSON
SYKES

1911
JACKSON
HARRISON
SHAW
WARD
WILKINSON
WATSON
BARKER

When King Richard II was overthrown in 1399, antagonism between the House of York and the House of Lancaster, both branches of the royal House of Plantagenet, began to emerge. Eventually the two houses fought for the throne of England in a series of civil wars, commonly known as the Wars of the Roses. Some of the battles took place in Yorkshire, such as those at Wakefield and Towton, the latter often regarded as the bloodiest battle ever fought on English soil.

The Dissolution of the Monasteries in 1536 led to a popular uprising known as the Pilgrimage of Grace, which started in Yorkshire as a protest. Some Catholics in Yorkshire continued to practise their religion and those caught were executed during the reign of Elizabeth I.

During the English Civil War, which started in 1642, Yorkshire had divided loyalties. York was a base for Royalists; while from their base in Hull the Parliamentarians fought back, taking Yorkshire town by town, until they won the Battle of Marston Moor and with it control of all of the north of England.

The wool textile industry has long been important to Yorkshire's economy. It began as a cottage industry centred on the old market towns, then moved to the West Riding where entrepreneurs were building mills that took advantage of water power gained by harnessing the rivers and ➤

Yorkshire (continued)

streams flowing from the Pennines. The developing textile industry helped Wakefield and Halifax grow. In the 16th and 17th centuries Leeds and other wool-focused towns continued to grow, along with Huddersfield, Hull and Sheffield, while coal mining first came into prominence in the West Riding.

Canals and turnpike roads were introduced in the late 18th century. In the following century, the spa towns of Harrogate and Scarborough flourished, due to people believing mineral water had curative properties.

The 19th century saw Yorkshire's continued growth, with the population growing and the Industrial Revolution continuing with prominent industries in coal, textile and steel (especially in Sheffield and Rotherham). However, despite the booming industry, living conditions declined in the industrial towns due to overcrowding – this saw bouts of cholera in both 1832 and 1848. Fortunately, advances were made by the end of the century with the introduction of modern sewers and water supplies. ⌧

RESOURCES

- North Yorkshire Record Office, Northallerton, www.northyorks.gov.uk/article/5173/County-record-office
- Sheffield Archives & Local Studies, www.sheffield.gov.uk/libraries/archives-and-local-studies.html
- East Riding Archives Service, Beverley, www2.eastriding.gov.uk/leisure/archives-family-and-local-history/
- West Yorkshire Archive Service (offices in Bradford, Calderdale, Kirklees, Leeds and Wakefield), www.archives.wyjs.org.uk
- York Libraries & Archives, https://www.exploreyork.org.uk/
- The Borthwick Institute for Archives, York, www.york.ac.uk/library/borthwick
- Yorkshire Archaeological Society – Family History Section, www.yorkshireroots.org.uk
- City of York & District Family History Society, www.yorkfamilyhistory.org.uk
- East Yorkshire FHS, www.eyfhs.org.uk
- Cleveland, North Yorkshire & South Durham FHS, www.clevelandfhs.org.uk
- Ryedale Family History Group, www.ryedalefamilyhistory.org
- Selby & District Family History Group,
- www.selbydistrictfamilyhistory.btck.co.uk
- Barnsley FHS, www.barnsleyfhs.co.uk
- Bradford FHS, www.bradfordfhs.org.uk
- Calderdale FHS, www.cfhsweb.com
- Doncaster & District Society for Family History, www.doncasterfhs.co.uk
- Harrogate & District FHS, www.hadfhs.co.uk
- Huddersfield & District FHS, www.hdfhs.org.uk
- Keighley & District FHS, www.kdfhs.org.uk
- Morley & District FHG, www.morleyfhg.co.uk
- Pontefract & District FHS, www.pontefractfhs.org.uk
- Ripon Historical Society & Family History Group, www.riponhistoricalsociety.org.uk
- Rotherham FHS, www.rotherhamfhs.co.uk
- Sheffield & District FHS, www.sheffieldfhs.org.uk
- Wakefield & District FHS, www.wdfhs.co.uk
- Wharfedale Family History Group, www.wharfedalefhg.org.uk
- The York Army Museum, www.yorkshireregiment.com/museum/
- The Green Howards Museum, Richmond, www.greenhowards.org.uk
- Find other resources at www.genuki.org.uk/big/eng/YKS/

Wales

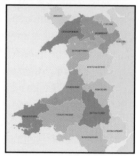

By the time of the Roman invasion of Britain, the area of modern Wales had been divided among the Celtic tribes of the Deceangli, Ordovices, Cornovii, Demetae and Silures for centuries. The Romans used their engineering technology to extract large amounts of gold, copper and lead, as well as modest amounts of some other metals such as zinc and silver.

By AD 500, the land that would become Wales had divided into a number of kingdoms free from Anglo-Saxon rule. By the 8th century, the eastern borders with the Anglo-Saxons had broadly been set, much of them marked by Offa's Dyke. The Anglo-Saxons called the Romano-British people 'Walha', meaning 'Romanised foreigner' – the Welsh continued to call themselves Brythoniaid (Brythons or Britons) well into the Middle Ages, though the first written evidence of the use of 'Cymru' is found in the 7th century.

A few years after the Battle of Hastings, William I established a series of lordships allocated to his most powerful warriors along the Welsh border. This frontier region became known as the Welsh Marches, in which the Marcher Lords were subject to neither English nor Welsh law. Edward I completed his conquest of Wales in 1282 and constructed a ➤

RECORDS

Wales records at TheGenealogist.co.uk:

- **Trade directories:** seven directories from 1835-1920.

- **Parish registers** for various parishes (see www.thegenealogist.co.uk/coverage/parish-records/) in Brecknockshire, Caernarfonshire, Flintshire and Monmouthshire, plus transcriptions for West Wales from 1910-11; the site's large collection of Nonconformist records includes many records from Wales.

- **Land owners:** tithe commutation records and some maps, plus records of Welsh landowners in 1873.

SURNAMES

Common Welsh names (excluding those most common in England as well, such as JONES):

1841	1911
MORGAN	LEWIS
REES	HUGHES
GRIFFITHS	MORGAN
JAMES	GRIFFITHS
PRICE	REES
JENKINS	JAMES
OWEN	JENKINS
MORRIS	OWEN
PARRY	PRICE
LLOYD	PHILLIPS
OWENS	MORRIS
	RICHARDS
	LLOYD

Wales (continued)

series of great stone castles at Beaumaris, Caernarfon and Conwy.

In 1404, Owain Glyndŵr led a major uprising against Henry IV and went on to hold parliamentary assemblies at several Welsh towns, including Machynlleth, but eventually went into hiding less than a decade later. The March of Wales was finally abolished under the formal Acts of Union in 1536.

Before the Industrial Revolution, there were signs of small-scale industries scattered throughout Wales. These ranged from industries connected to agriculture, such as milling and the manufacture of woollen textiles, through to mining and quarrying.

The industrial period began around the development of copper smelting in the Swansea area. With access to local coal deposits and a harbour that could take advantage of Cornwall's copper mines and the deposits being extracted from the then largest copper mine in the world at Parys Mountain on Anglesey, Swansea developed into the world's major centre for non-ferrous metal smelting in the 19th century. The second metal industry to expand in Wales was iron smelting, and iron manufacturing became prevalent in both the north and the south of the country. In the 1820s, south Wales alone accounted for 40% of all pig iron manufactured in Britain.

In the late 18th century, slate quarrying began to expand rapidly, most notably in north Wales. By the late 19th century, Penrhyn Quarry was employing 15,000 men. Meanwhile coal mining became synonymous with Wales and its people. Initially, coal seams were exploited to provide energy for local metal industries but, with the opening of canal systems and later

COUNTIES OF WALES

- The historic counties of Wales (with Welsh names in brackets) are: Anglesey (Sir Fôn), Brecknockshire (Sir Frycheiniog), Caernarfonshire (Sir Gaernarfon), Cardiganshire (Sir Aberteifi or Ceredigion), Carmarthenshire (Sir Gaerfyrddin or Sir Gâr), Denbighshire (Sir Ddinbych), Flintshire (Sir y Fflint), Glamorganshire (Sir Forgannwg or Morgannwg), Merionethshire (Sir Feirionnydd or Meirionnydd), Montgomeryshire (Sir Drefaldwyn), Monmouthshire (Sir Fynwy), Pembrokeshire (Sir Benfro), Radnorshire (Sir Faesyfed).
- The Counties (Detached Parts) Act 1844 abolished several enclaves. One of these, Welsh Bicknor (Llangystennin) was an exclave of Monmouthshire between Gloucestershire and Herefordshire and was transferred to Herefordshire. Another was Ffwddog, identified using the English variant Fothock on older maps, an exclave of Herefordshire transferred to Monmouthshire. The exclave of Flintshire, called Maelor Saesneg (English Maelor) was, however, left untouched.
- The 'preserved counties' of Wales, still used for ceremonial purposes and some based on ancient Welsh kingdoms, date from 1972 (used administratively until 1996). They are: Clwyd, Dyfed, Gwent, Gwynedd , Mid Glamorgan, Powys, South Glamorgan, West Glamorgan.

RESOURCES

• Find archives in Wales via Archives Wales, www.archiveswales.org.uk
• National Library of Wales, Aberystwyth, www.llgc.org.uk
• Gwynedd Family History Society, www.gwyneddfhs.org
• Powys FHS, www.rootsweb.com/~wlspfhs
• Cardiganshire FHS, www.cgnfhs.org.uk
• Dyfed FHS, www.dyfedfhs.org.uk
• Clwyd FHS, www.clwydfhs.org.uk
• Glamorgan FHS, www.glamfhs.org.uk
• Gwent FHS, www.gwentfhs.org.uk
• Montgomeryshire Genealogical Society, www.montgomeryshiregs.org.uk
• The Regimental Museum of the Royal Welsh, Brecon, www.royalwelsh.org.uk
• Firing Line (Cardiff Castle Museum of the Welsh Soldier), www.cardiffcastlemuseum.org.uk
• Royal Welch Fusiliers Museum, Caernarfon Castle, www.rwfmuseum.org.uk
• Find other resources at www.genuki.org.uk/big/wal

the railways, Welsh coal mining saw a boom in its demand.

As the south Wales coalfield was exploited, mainly in the upland valleys around Aberdare and later the Rhondda, the ports of Swansea, Cardiff and later Penarth grew into world exporters of coal and, with them, came a population boom. By its height in 1913, Wales was producing almost 61 million tons of coal. There was also a significant coalfield in the north-east of the country, particularly around Wrexham.

A total of 272,924 Welshmen served in World War One, representing 21.5% of the male population. Of these, roughly 35,000 were killed, many at the Somme and Passchendaele.

In 1916, David Lloyd George became the first Welshman to become Prime Minister of Britain, but his poor handling of the 1919 coalminers' strike was a key factor in destroying support for the Liberal party in south Wales. The industrial workers of Wales began shifting towards a new political organisation, now called the Labour Party, which dominated Wales for decades thereafter.

Despite economic growth in the first two decades of the 20th century, from the early 1920s to the late 1930s, Wales's staple industries endured a prolonged slump, leading to widespread unemployment and poverty in the South Wales valleys. In World War Two, after 1943, 10% of Welsh conscripts aged 18 were sent to work in the coal mines to rectify labour shortages; they became known as Bevin Boys.

The 20th century also saw a revival in Welsh national feeling, with nationalist party Plaid Cymru formed in 1925, and rapid growth in Welsh speaking after many years of decline. ✠

Scotland

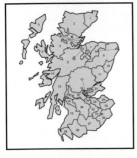

The Kingdom of the Picts was the state that eventually became known as 'Alba' or 'Scotland'. By the 12th century, the kings of Alba had added to their territories the English-speaking land in the south-east and attained overlordship of Gaelic-speaking Galloway and Norse-speaking Caithness; by the end of the 13th century, the kingdom had assumed approximately its modern borders.

Feudalism, government reorganisation and the first legally recognised towns (called burghs) began in the 12th century. Influenced by Anglo-French knights, the culture and language of the low-lying and coastal parts of the kingdom's original territory in the east became English-speaking, while the rest of the country retained the Gaelic language, apart from the Northern Isles of Orkney and Shetland, which remained under Norse rule until 1468.

The Scottish state entered a largely successful and stable period between the 12th and 14th centuries, there was relative peace with England, and trade and educational links were well developed with the Continent.

The death of Alexander III in 1286 broke the centuries-old succession line of Scotland's kings. Edward I of England was asked to arbitrate between claimants for the Scottish crown, and John Balliol was pronounced king in

COUNTIES OF SCOTLAND

(Numbers refer to map above)

• Counties before 1890: 1. Caithness 2.Sutherland 3.Ross 4.Cromarty 5.Inverness 6.Nairn 7.Elgin 8.Banff 9.Aberdeen 10.Kincardine 11.Forfar 12.Perth 13.Argyll 14.Bute 15.Ayr 16.Renfrew 17.Dumbarton 18.Stirling 19.Clackmannan 20.Kinross 21.Fife 22.Linlithgow 23.Edinburgh 24.Haddington 25.Berwick 26.Roxburgh 27.Dumfries 28.Kirkcudbright 29. Wigtown 30. Lanark 31.Selkirk 32.Peebles. Not shown on map: Zetland (Shetland), Orkney

• Counties from 1890-1975: Aberdeen, Angus (County of Forfar until 1928), Argyll, Ayr, Banffshire, Berwick, Bute, Caithness, Clackmannan, Dumfries, Dunbarton, East Lothian (County of Haddington until 1921), Fife, Inverness, Kincardineshire, Kinross, Kirkcudbright, Lanark, Midlothian (County of Edinburgh until 1890), Moray (County of Elgin until 1918), Nairn, Orkney, Peebles, Perth, Renfrew, Ross and Cromarty, Roxburgh, Selkirk, Stirling, Sutherland, West Lothian (County of Linlithgow until 1924), Wigtown, Zetland (Shetland)

• Local government areas from 1973 to 1996: Borders, Central, Dumfries and Galloway, Fife, Grampian, Highland, Lothian, Orkney, Shetland, Strathclyde, Tayside, Western Isles.

RECORDS

Scottish records at TheGenealogist.co.uk:
- **Trade directories:** directories for Aberdeen, Edinburgh, Glasgow, Greenock, Perthshire, Orkney and Shetland.
- **Parish registers** for Torphichen, Durness, Restalrig and Haddington.
- **Land owners:** a directory of landowners in 1872-73.
- **University registers** for Glasgow and Aberdeen.
- Burgesses of Edinburgh 1406-1700.
- A collection of 17th century Edinburgh **wills**.
- Records of the Scots **Navy** from 1689 to 1710.
- Some **census** records for 1851.

SURNAMES

Common Scottish names in 1901:

SMITH	BROWN
ROBERTSON	WILSON
CAMPBELL	THOMSON
STEWART	ANDERSON
MCDONALD	SCOTT
REID	MURRAY
ROSS	FRASER
YOUNG	CLARK
TAYLOR	MITCHELL
HENDERSON	CAMERON
WATSON	PATERSON
MCKENZIE	MORRISON
WALKER	DAVIDSON
MILLER	MCLEAN
DUNCAN	GRAY

1292. Edward steadily undermined his authority. In 1294, Balliol and other Scottish lords refused Edward's demands to serve in his army against the French; Scotland and France sealed a treaty in 1295, known as the Auld Alliance. War ensued and King John was deposed by Edward who took personal control of Scotland. Andrew Moray and William Wallace initially emerged as the principal leaders of the resistance to English rule in what became known as the Wars of Scottish Independence (1296–1328).

In the early 14th century Robert the Bruce battled to restore Scottish independence, gradually winning Scotland back from the Norman English invaders, with victory at the Battle of Bannockburn in 1314. However, war with England continued for several decades after the death of Bruce.

The Stuarts ruled Scotland for the remainder of the Middle Ages. The country they ruled experienced greater prosperity from the end of the 14th century through the Scottish Renaissance to the Reformation. This was despite continual warfare with England, and the increasing division between Highlands and Lowlands,.

In 1502, James IV of Scotland signed the Treaty of Perpetual Peace with Henry VII of England, and married Henry's daughter. A decade later, James made the fateful decision to invade England in support of France under the terms of the Auld Alliance. He was the last British monarch to die in battle, at the Battle of Flodden.

In 1560, John Knox realised his goal of seeing Scotland become a Protestant nation and the Scottish parliament revoke papal authority in ➤

Scotland (continued)

Scotland. Mary, Queen of Scots, a Catholic and former queen of France, was forced to abdicate in 1567.

In 1603, James VI, King of Scots inherited the thrones of the Kingdom of England and the Kingdom of Ireland, and became King James I of England and Ireland, leaving Edinburgh for London. With the exception of a short period under the Protectorate, Scotland remained a separate state, but there was considerable conflict between the crown and the Covenanters over the form of church government. In the 1690s, Scotland experienced famine, which reduced the population of parts of the country by at least 20%.

On 22 July 1706, the Treaty of Union was agreed between representatives of the Scots Parliament and the Parliament of England and the following year twin Acts of Union were passed to create the united Kingdom of Great Britain. Scotland remained independent in many ways. Following the union, the country maintained its own separate legal system of Scots Law, its own education system and its own state church. As a result, Scottish family history records tend to be very different to those found elsewhere in the British Isles.

The civil registration of Scottish births, marriages and deaths, for example, started in 1855, 18 years after England – but the records hold much more information than their English and Welsh counterparts, such as the names of both parents (including maiden name) in each. The land system of feudalism in England and Wales, with 'vassals' holding land of their 'superiors', was abolished in medieval times, but governed virtually every land transfer in Scotland until its abolition in 2004. And where the state church in England, Wales and Ireland was the Anglican Church, adminis-tered by bishops and archbishops etc, the Scottish 'Kirk' had no bishops at all for most of its existence, with congregations instead democratically electing their own ministers. Scotland was one of the main powerhouses of the Industrial Revolution in Britain, but prior to the invention of steam power was largely rural. People worked on their own plots of land as well as that of their laird, or put themselves out for hire for set periods at the Scottish term days of Whitsun and Martinmas. To the north of the Highland line, the Gaelic-speaking clans lived in small separate territories under the protection of a clan chief. Those in the more urbanised population lived in the main trading burghs of the Scots-speaking central belt and eastern coast, working as craftsmen and merchants, and with constant contact with their English neighbours. The inhabitants of the Lowlands and the Highlands regarded each as other as foreigners and with much suspicion.

Several major developments changed the country by the end of the 17th century and early 18th. The union was not popular with the common folk of the country, who saw it as a means for the Scottish nobility to advance themselves at the people's expense. With strong support from the peoples of the Highlands, there were several Jacobite rebellions in the first half of the 18th century to try to restore the power of the Stuarts. With their failure the clan system breathed its last, with the resultant pacification of the Highlands. Many of the chiefs then adopted the idea of trying to make money from their lands rather than protect the clans to which they were supposed to give a lead. Thousands of people were forced from their homes into exile during what became known as the 'clearances', and in their wake came more profitable sheep.

In the southern half of the country a different story would unfold. Vast open estates were enclosed into more efficient farms, and many former agricultural labourers flocked to the big cities to seek work. As the Industrial Revolution took a hold, coal and iron ore was mined in Ayrshire, Lanarkshire and Fife, while textiles mills were established in Glasgow, Perth and Dundee. Navvies carved out an infrastructure of canals and then built the railways and, on the Clyde, John Brown's shipyard workers built a fleet for the rapidly growing British Empire, first from wood and then of iron.

As the country grew, the church's structure of parishes found it hard to cope with the expansion of the major cities. There were regular disagreements about the role of the state and the role of landowners in the affairs of the Kirk. During the 18th and 19th centuries various wings split from the establishment, the most important being in 1843 when a third of the Kirk's ministers walked away to form the Free Church of Scotland. The role of the Kirk itself declined in everyday life, and the various roles it once had were gradually transferred to the state, such as education, discipline and the administration of poor relief. 🏴

RESOURCES

- National Records of Scotland, Edinburgh, www.nrscotland.gov.uk
- Mitchell Library, Glasgow, www.glasgowfamilyhistory.org.uk
- National Library of Scotland, Edinburgh, www.nls.uk
- Find research groups via the Scottish Association of Family History Societies, www.safhs.org.uk/members.asp
- National War Museum, Edinburgh, www.nms.ac.uk/national-war-museum
- The Royal Scots Museum, Edinburgh, www.theroyalscots.co.uk/page/museum/
- Find other resources at www.genuki.org.uk/big/sct

Northern Ireland

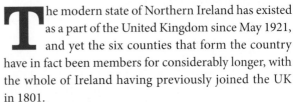

The modern state of Northern Ireland has existed as a part of the United Kingdom since May 1921, and yet the six counties that form the country have in fact been members for considerably longer, with the whole of Ireland having previously joined the UK in 1801.

The influence of Britain in Ireland goes back to Norman times, but it was from the early 1600s that waves of Scots and English people were physically settled by the British Crown in the north of the island, in an effort to pacify the region towards Crown influence. The most significant factor from this 'plantation' was that these new colonists were followers of Britain's Protestant reformed religions, while the majority of the island's population, as to this day, adhered strongly to the Roman Catholic faith.

Following the political and sectarian turmoil within the country between 1916 and 1921 (which included the Easter Rising in Dublin and the Anglo-Irish War), an imperfect solution was found by partitioning the island into two new states. Northern Ireland was founded with a predominantly Protestant-based population, and in the south the Irish Free State was largely Catholic, later to become a fully fledged republic. It should be noted that as well as Ireland being divided, so too was the historic province of Ulster – counties Antrim, Down, Armagh, Tyrone, Fermanagh and Londonderry remained within the British union, while counties Donegal, Monaghan and Cavan were included within the southern state.

For family historians this divided history provides some interesting challenges, none more so than overcoming the destruction of a significant proportion of the island's official records in Dublin during the south's subsequent civil war in 1922, by a faction of the IRA which did not agree with partition. In the years following this act of vandalism, many good people on both sides of the Irish border have retrieved much of the genealogical information lost from copies of records that were preserved through chance, or through materials fortunately not held at the Public Record Office when it was destroyed. Despite a great deal of information being still lost forever, where there is the will to get through

RECORDS

Irish records at TheGenealogist.co.uk:

- **Trade directories:** 11 directories for Ireland from 1899-1927, including 1905 and 1926 directories for Belfast, and a 1905 one for Ulster.

- **Land owners:** a directory of landowners in Ireland (including what is now Northern Ireland) in 1876.

- **Griffith's Valuation** of Ireland 1847-1864.

SURNAMES

Common Irish names in 1890:

All of Ireland	Province of Ulster
MURPHY	GALLAGHER
KELLY	DOHERTY
O'SULLIVAN	REILLY
WALSH	SMITH
SMITH	JOHNSTON
O'BRIEN	STEWART
BYRNE	WILSON
RYAN	BOYLE
O'CONNOR	O'DONNELL
O'NEILL	THOMPSON

RESOURCES

- Public Record Office of Northern Ireland, Belfast, www.proni.gov.uk
- General Register Office Northern Ireland, Belfast, https://geni.nidirect.gov.uk
- North of Ireland Family History Society, www.nifhs.org
- Royal Irish Fusiliers Museum, Armagh, www.royal-irish.com/museums/royal-irish-fusiliers-museum
- Royal Ulster Rifles Museum, Belfast, www.royal-irish.com/museums/royal-ulster-rifles-museum
- Find other resources at www.genuki.org.uk/big/eng/irl

a particular brick wall, very often there may still be a way.

Prior to May 1921, the administrative centre for Ireland was based in Dublin but, following the island's division, Belfast became the capital of the north. This means that for Northern Irish research you will often have to consult resources in both cities, as well as from more localised holdings.

As with any genealogy research, it all starts with the vital records of births, marriages and deaths. State-based registration commenced in April 1845, but only for non-Roman Catholic based church marriages, or through civil marriages performed by a registrar (which could include Roman Catholics). It was not until January 1864 that civil records for all births, death and marriages (for all denominations) were gathered by the General Register Office (GRO) in Dublin.

Most census records prior to 1901 have unfortunately been destroyed, but those from 1901 and 1911 have been digitised by the National Archives of Ireland, and made freely available online through its genealogy records platform at www.genealogy.nationalarchives.ie. Some remnants before this do survive – the 1851 census for a significant part of County Antrim, for example, is transcribed and available online. ✖

Channel Islands

The Channel Islands have a long and colourful history. Neolithic farmers settled c5000BC and created the many dolmens and menhirs found in the islands. Christianity arrived in the 6th century. In 933 the islands came under the control of the Duchy of Normandy, and today the Channel Islands represent the medieval duchy's last remnants remaining to England.

The islands were repeatedly attacked by French pirates and naval forces in the Middle Ages. During the English Civil War, Jersey remained Royalist while Guernsey sided with Parliament.

The islands prospered during the 18th and 19th centuries due to their success in the global maritime trade and the rise of the stone industry.

Since earliest times the islands have had a migrant population. In the early part of the 19th century, the majority of islanders still spoke a Franco-Norman dialect with a culture related to their close French neighbours. This changed dramatically around the time of WWI when the islands became influenced by the English economy and culture.

From around 1600, some islanders left their homes for new lives in North America, Australia, New Zealand and other far-flung places. Sir Walter Raleigh was the Governor of Jersey in the early 1600s and his interest in the development of Newfoundland and Virginia focused islanders' attention on the New World.

Likewise, immigrants have always come to the islands looking for work. A study of the Guernsey censuses from 1841 to 1901 gives the number of English immigrants as just over 20,000, followed by French immigrants at just over 4,000 and Irish at 2,500. Many of these immigrants to Guernsey would have worked in the stone trade. Guernsey granite was used to pave London streets from 1823 (and Jersey granite was used for Chatham docks). Sizeable building projects in the islands drew a large immigrant labour force who worked on the building of the harbours in St Helier in Jersey and St Peter Port in Guernsey as well as the Alderney breakwater, St Catherine's breakwater in Jersey and the building of military forts.

The first Jersey Royal potato was grown in 1872 and this industry has always attracted migrant workers right up to today. Other trades in the islands over the centuries have included knitting (Guernsey stockings were said to be worn by Queen Elizabeth I, and Jersey sweaters are famous), ship-

RECORDS

Channel Islands records at
TheGenealogist.co.uk:
• **Census** records from 1841 to 1911.
• **Trade directories:** Channel Islands
directories for 1899 and 1911
• **Nonconformist registers** for Jersey.
• A detailed database of **headstones**
which include photographs.
• The Channel Island Monthly Review
covering the **occupation**.

SURNAMES

Common Channel Islands names:

1841	1911
MANGER	RENOUF
LE PAGE	HAMON
AMY	MAUGER
MARTIN	FALLA
ROBERT	MAHY
HAMON	BISSON
SIMON	NICOLLE
LANGLOIS	CARRE

RESOURCES

• Jersey Archive, www.jerseyheritage.org/places-to-visit/jersey-archive
• Jersey Library, www.gov.je/Leisure/Libraries/Pages/OtherServices.aspx
• The Greffe, www.guernseyroyalcourt.gg
• The Priaulx Library, www.priaulxlibrary.co.uk
• Guernsey Archives, www.gov.gg/islandarchives
• Channel Islands Family History Society, www.jerseyfamilyhistory.org
• The Société Jersiaise, www.societe-jersiaise.org/library/
• The Guernsey Society, www.guernsey-society.org.uk
• La Société Guernesiaise, www.societe.org.gg
• Alderney Greffe, http://alderney.gov.gg/article/110418/Greffier-of-the-Court
• Sark Greffe, www.gov.sark.gg
• La Société Sercquaise, www.socsercq.sark.gg
• Channel Islands Military Museum, www.jersey.com/english/sightsandactivities/attractions/attractions/Pages/channelislandsmilitarymuseum.aspx
• Find other resources at http://chi.genuki.weald.org.uk

building, fishing, agriculture and horticulture and of course the trades which support the population: butchers, shoemakers, seamstresses, gardeners etc. Grapes were grown in glasshouses from about 1860 and then tomatoes. The tomato industry became very successful and at its height in the late 1960s nearly half a billion tomatoes were picked yearly and exported to England.

During World War One thousands of island men served in the British Army in France. There were heavy losses with around 1,200 Jersey men and 1,000 Guernsey men not returning. The islands were then occupied by German troops in World War Two. Many islanders were evacuated to England just before the arrival of the German forces and some were deported by the Germans to camps in the southwest of Germany. There was a concentration camp in Alderney occupied by forced labourers from Eastern Europe. The islands were heavily fortified during WWII as part of Hitler's Atlantic Wall and defences are still visible all around the coast today. ⊞

Isle of Man

The earliest traces of people on the Isle of Man (also known as Mann) date back to the Middle Stone Age. The Iron Age marked the beginning of Celtic cultural influence. Large hill forts appeared on hill summits and smaller promontory forts along the coastal cliffs, while large timber-framed roundhouses were built. It is generally assumed that Irish invasion or immigration formed the basis of the modern Manx language; Irish migration to the island probably began in the 5th century AD. Tradition attributes the island's conversion to Christianity to St Maughold (Maccul), an Irish missionary.

Between about 800 and 815 the Vikings came to Mann chiefly for plunder; between 850 and 990, when they settled in it, the island fell under the rule of the Scandinavian Kings of Dublin; and between 990 and 1079 it became subject to the powerful Earls of Orkney. The conqueror Godred Crovan created the Kingdom of Mann and the Isles in around 1079; it included the southwestern islands of Scotland (Sodor) until 1164, when two separate kingdoms were formed from it. In 1154, the Diocese of Sodor and Man was formed under the Church of England. During the whole of the Scandinavian period, the isle remained nominally under the the Kings of Norway. In 1266 King Magnus VI of Norway ceded Mann to Scotland in the Treaty of Perth.

The island's parliament, Tynwald, has been in continuous existence since AD 979 or earlier, making it the oldest continuously governing body in the world.

In 1290 King Edward I of England sent Walter de Huntercombe to take possession of Mann, and it remained in English hands until 1313, when Robert Bruce took it after besieging Castle Rushen for five weeks. There followed a confused period when Mann sometimes experienced English rule and sometimes Scottish. In 1399 the island came into the possession of the English Crown.

Henry IV, in 1405, made a lifetime grant of it to Sir John Stanley, and 13 members of his family ruled in Mann until the 18th century other than a brief gap after the English Civil War.

RESOURCES

- Public Record Office, Douglas,
  www.gov.im/pro
- Civil Registry, Douglas,
  www.gov.im/registries/general/
  civilregistry/welcome.xml
- Manx National Heritage,
  www.manxnationalheritage.im
- Isle of Man Family History Society,
  www.iomfhs.im
- Manx Aviation and Military Museum,
  Ballasalla, www.visitisleofman.com/
  placestovisit/museums/aviation.xml
- Isle of Man census records are available
  at www.thegenealogist.co.uk
- Find other resources at
  www.genuki.org.uk/big/iom

SURNAMES

Common Manx names:

1841	1911
KELLY	KELLY
QUAYLE	QUAYLE
CORLETT	CORLETT
CHRISTIAN	MOORE
CAIN	CHRISTIAN
MOORE	CLAGUE
CLAGUE	CAIN
KNEALE	SHIMMIN
COWLEY	WATTERSON
CANNELL	KNEALE
CUBBON	CORKILL
QUIRK	QUIRK
BRIDSON	CANNELL
KEWLEY	COWIN

In the 18th century, during the rule of James Murray, 2nd Duke of Atholl, and his son-in-law, the British parliament passed legislation to curb the contraband trade flourishing on Mann.

Agriculture was long in a low condition on the island, but improved in the 18th century. Its crops have included wheat, beans, barley, oats and potatoes. Seaweed was largely used for manure. Fishing, particularly for herring, cod, ling and lobster, has long been central to the island's economy, exported to both Ireland and England.

Manufacture has been minimal, but woollen goods were produced in the mills of Braddan; sailcloths, ropes, and nets, largely at Tromade, near Douglas; paper, soap, and starch, at Laxey and Sulby Glen; and iron ware, at Douglas.

Since 1866, the Isle of Man has been a Crown Dependency and has had democratic self-government. Since then Mann has thrived as an offshore financial centre, as well as from its tourist industry, which began in the 1820s although declined in the mid-20th century.

The Isle of Man was a base for alien civilian internment camps in both world wars. The (now disbanded) Manx Regiment was raised in 1938 and saw action during World War Two.

The early 20th century saw a revival of music, dance, and a limited revival of the Manx language, although the last 'native' speaker of Manx Gaelic died in the 1970s. The 1960s also saw a rise in Manx nationalism. In 1973, control of the postal service passed from the UK General Post Office to the new Isle of Man Post, which began to issue its own postage stamps. ⚔